Praise for *The Non Nonprofit*

"Steve Rothschild's fresh thinking translates proven strategies that successful businesses employ every day into practical approaches to confronting centuries-old issues like poverty. No partisan politics, no fancy tricks—just fundamental, time-tested solutions."

> —**Harvey Mackay,** author, *Swim With The Sharks Without Being Eaten Alive*

"As a Twin Cities RISE! customer, I can say unequivocally that the seven principles in *The Non Nonprofit* work. RISE! provides just the type of employee that every company needs to be successful: self-motivated, engaged, skilled, productive, and emotionally mature. The employer community would do well to take much greater advantage of this underutilized organization."

> —**David Abrams**, vice president, North Memorial Health Care

"I've observed from the beginning of his anti-poverty work Steve Rothschild's efforts to put his principles into practice. I've observed with the skeptical eye of an evaluator. I've seen hundreds of good ideas and hopeful visions flounder in the face of complex realities. I'm not easily impressed. But what Rothschild has accomplished impresses. The principles he identifies, explains, and illustrates have broad applicability. He has learned a great deal about what works. Anyone who cares about making a difference should pay attention to what he's learned—it's all here."

> —**Michael Quinn Patton**, founder and director, Utilization-Focused Evaluation; former president, American Evaluation Association

"As director of the U.S. Agency for International Development (USAID) for six years in the 1990s, I presided over the U.S. government's global poverty reduction efforts. Steve Rothschild reminds me of the innovators whose practical approaches changed the world of development, people like Hernando De Soto and Muhammad Yunus. Rothschild understands incentives, accountability, and personal improvement. His Twin Cities RISE! is a learning-driven organization that empowers challenged citizens to overcome their issues and succeed. Rothschild's RISE! is not afraid to establish a bottom line and is eager to be held accountable for achieving it. *The Non Nonprofit* and its recipes for success are a must-read for those who are truly concerned about poverty, here or anywhere."

> **—J. Brian Atwood,** former dean, Humphrey School of Public Affairs, University of Minnesota; chair, Development Assistance Committee, Organization for Economic Co-operation and Development

"I take pride in being one of the many people Steve Rothschild met and talked with when he was first thinking of starting what turned out to be Twin Cities RISE! I must admit that while I thought his market-based approach was exquisitely on target, I was concerned he wasn't giving adequate weight to the many attitudinal and behavioral shortcomings that keep large numbers of people impoverished. More than fifteen years later, it's clear I was wrong, as I know of no analyst or practitioner in the United States who better understands how efforts to help poor people must meld both economically grounded and culturally grounded approaches."

> **—Mitch Pearlstein**, founder and CEO, Center for the American Experiment

THE NON NONPROFIT

FOR-PROFIT THINKING FOR NONPROFIT SUCCESS

Steve Rothschild

Foreword by Bill George

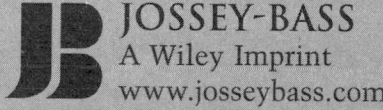

JOSSEY-BASS
A Wiley Imprint
www.josseybass.com

Published by Jossey-Bass
A Wiley Imprint
One Montgomery Street, Suite 1200, San Francisco, CA 94104-4594
www.josseybass.com

Jossey-Bass books and products are available through most bookstores. To
contact Jossey-Bass directly call our Customer Care Department within the U.S.
at 800-956-7739, outside the U.S. at 317-572-3986, or fax 317-572-4002.

Wiley publishes in a variety of print and electronic formats and by print-on-
demand. Some material included with standard print versions of this book may not
be included in e-books or in print-on-demand. If this book refers to media such as
a CD or DVD that is not included in the version you purchased, you may
download this material at http://booksupport.wiley.com. For more information
about Wiley products, visit www.wiley.com.

Library of Congress Cataloging-in-Publication Data

Rothschild, Steve.
    The non nonprofit : for-profit thinking for nonprofit success / Steve Rothschild;
foreword by Bill George. —1st ed.
        p. cm.
    Includes bibliographical references and index.
    ISBN 978-1-118-02181-1 (cloth); ISBN 978-1-118-18020-4 (ebk);
ISBN 978-1-118-18021-1 (ebk); ISBN 978-1-118-18022-8 (ebk)
    1. Nonprofit organizations—Management. I. Title.
    HD62.6.R68 2012
    658'.048—dc23
                            2011041307

Printed in the United States of America

FIRST EDITION

HB Printing   10 9 8 7 6 5 4 3 2 1

For my wife, Marilyn,
whose love, dedication, and encouragement
have sustained me for fifty years

Contents

Foreword

How This Book
Will Benefit Us All

How many highly successful corporate executives walk away from a top job in midcareer to devote themselves to reducing poverty in our crime-ridden American inner cities? Steve Rothschild is the only one I know. He left a senior executive role at General Mills, spent a year studying the twin problems of racism and inner-city poverty, and then used his own money to found Twin Cities RISE!

I first met Steve in 1980 when we were together at a Berlitz class as he was building the Yoplait yogurt business for General Mills. Steve impressed me with his passion and his persistence, qualities that are writ large throughout this book. For years we challenged each other on the tennis court, talked between sets about our dreams of running a major company that could help people, and shared the frustrations we faced in our work.

One day I called Steve to tell him I had decided to join Medtronic, thinking my long-time friend would be enthusiastic about my move. When I shared my good news, there was a long silence at the other end of the phone. Confused, I asked Steve what he was feeling. After a long pause, he said, "I wish I was moving on as well." Steve confided that he was no longer inspired by his work and was feeling restless to do something more meaningful with his life.

So I wasn't surprised a few months later when he called to say he had resigned from General Mills. I immediately assumed he would move into a top corporate job at another company, a destiny that was clearly in his grasp. Instead, like the farmer who lets his fields go fallow for a season, Steve used the next year to get closer to his family and explore challenges in the Minneapolis community.

One day while serving on the Minneapolis Initiative Against Racism, Steve wondered what it must be like for an inner-city youth who was flipping hamburgers for a living. What hope did he have of making something of his life, of escaping from a dead-end job? Rothschild resolved then to explore the twin issues of poverty and racism in much greater depth to see what could be done about them.

In these pages, Rothschild shares what he has learned about the most intractable problem in our society today: the poverty concentrated in our inner cities that leads to the downward cycle of failure, hopelessness, despair, violence, crime, and eventually prison—and then repeats itself across generations. It is not a problem that many Americans want to address. Long ago the politicians stopped talking about the problems of the poor and started focusing primarily on the middle class.

Instead of rushing headlong into these problems with quick-fix solutions, Rothschild studied them carefully and talked to countless people in Minnesota and elsewhere about what could be done to correct them. His explorations led him to found Twin Cities RISE! It is based on the bedrock principles of creating value for employers and society to enable the poorest of the poor to qualify for jobs that pay more than $10 per hour.

To make RISE! successful, Rothschild focused all his energies on his new organization, using funds from his personal savings. Applying his enormous leadership and executive talents, he helped the inner-city poor who wrestle daily with the twin problems of discrimination and poverty to rise above their wounds and find a purpose for their lives. In so doing, Steve and RISE! (and RISE!'s graduates) faced the ravages of generational poverty head-on, encountered their ugliest aspects, and found a way to wrestle them to the ground.

RISE! is not just another social service agency that provides education and training programs for hard-to-employ individuals. It is also a success story that demonstrates the benefits of a new approach to addressing our social ills—one that applies sound capitalistic principles, like value creation and return on investment, to enable the most economically challenged citizens to achieve economic self-sufficiency.

Achieving success with RISE! hasn't been easy for Rothschild. Through his experiences, he's learned that preparing people for good jobs takes a lot more than skills training. First, the students have to face their own life stories, crucibles, and lack of self-worth head-on in order to then gain self-awareness and empowerment. Rothschild has also found it difficult to convince employers of the value that RISE! graduates offer them.

As he realized his goals locally with Twin Cities RISE! Rothschild began to focus on using these experiences to create a national model for addressing our social ills. *The Non Nonprofit* sets forth that model in a clear way and demonstrates how we can attack the greatest problems of our society and our world.

In visiting the Minneapolis offices of Twin Cities RISE! I discovered the remarkable parallels between Rothschild's work in preparing its students for good jobs and my own work in enabling leaders in corporations to step up to important leadership roles. Before they can become fully effective, both groups have to deal with their crucibles and past wounds, discover the passion for their purpose, become empowered, accept personal accountability for results, and continue to learn from their experiences, all based on a sound set of economic principles.

As Steve Rothschild demonstrates, this is not an easy process, and there is no such thing as five easy steps to economic self-sufficiency. But these commonsense principles will improve the results of any nonprofit, or for-profit for that matter, whether it is struggling or performing well. They will help sharpen an organization's focus, strengthen its organizational culture, and improve its results.

In this marvelous book, Steve Rothschild shares the same sound business principles he used at General Mills and later to found two nonprofits. Every social enterprise can benefit from these rigorous, real-world approaches, whether applied to traditional nonprofit organizations, philanthropy, or government. *The Non Nonprofit* brings to life this unique twenty-first-century approach to solving our social problems across America, and policymakers, politicians, and all others who want to build a more productive and just society ought to study it carefully.

Minneapolis, Minnesota   Bill George
December 2011

Bill George is professor of management practice at Harvard Business School and the author of *True North: Discover Your Authentic Leadership*. He is the former chairman and CEO of Medtronic, Inc.

THE NON NONPROFIT

Introduction

Historically, the most common response to social ills like poverty, homelessness, and poor education has been to spend more money. When money is tight, concerned citizens ramp up their efforts for more fundraising, more requests for federal grants and government funding, and, ultimately, more investment in short-term solutions to solve long-term problems. But these traditional efforts rarely yield sustainable long-term results. To make progress, leaders—in government, funding organizations, business, nonprofits, and social enterprise—need a new approach. They need an approach that integrates the best ideas of social programming with the expertise that the for-profit sector has acquired in achieving long-term outcomes. This book presents seven principles that equip leaders to do just that. These principles have demonstrated their ability to build healthy, effective organizations in both the for-profit and nonprofit sectors. Now we need to put them to work so that all organizations that strive to improve the social good can thrive through good economic times and bad.

These principles provide guidance for everything from strategic planning to organizational culture to policies, procedures, and programming. Organizations can, and should, adapt all of these activities as they respond to the world in which they operate and thereby grow and learn. These proven business principles remain steadfast, providing solid, unwavering direction that leads to positive, long-term results.

I began developing the seven principles during a twenty-two-year career in corporate America that led to an executive position at General Mills, a Fortune 100 company. Then I established Twin Cities RISE! (Responsible, Independent, Skilled, Employed) in the Minneapolis and St. Paul metropolitan area of Minnesota, a nonprofit dedicated to reducing poverty through job training, and I confirmed just how powerful these same principles are when applied to social issues. *The Non Nonprofit* describes exactly how the principles have contributed to successful outcomes at RISE! and how they strengthen social enterprises in the United States and around the rest of the world. (By social enterprise, I mean an organization that takes a business approach to attacking social problems regardless of whether the organization operates as a for-profit or nonprofit entity.) *The Non Nonprofit* poses questions to help leaders understand how the seven principles apply to their organizations. The book shows you how your organization can improve results for your clients and for society by putting these time-tested for-profit principles into practice.

WHY THE SEVEN PRINCIPLES ARE SO IMPORTANT NOW

The United States urgently needs more effective enterprises dedicated to solving our social ills. Voices from the private sector, philanthropy, foundations, and state and national governments are all demanding greater productivity from our social-purpose organizations. In addition, although the recession of 2009 is easing as I write in 2011, it's likely that government funding for many social programs will continue to decline despite an economic recovery.

One major reason is that health care costs are expected to grow at twice the rate of state revenue growth over the next twenty years. This is driven in part by an aging population that uses more health care and in part by spiraling health care costs. As a result, state budgets will have significantly fewer resources available for human services other than health care and K-12 education. At the federal level, virtually all the resources will be put toward social security, Medicare, Medicaid, interest on the debt, and defense. There will be little left for anything else. The "discretionary" programs that provide a better quality of life for individuals and society will suffer greatly.

These are programs like drug treatment, workforce development, higher education, and early childhood education—investments that promote long-term social and economic growth. Many of these programs are preventative, and they cost less than addressing the problem at the back end. Given this funding situation, it's imperative that we become more productive in how we spend our money in nonprofits and social enterprises and do a better job of attracting new capital to these enterprises.

The seven principles set out in this book can enable us to do both. Twin Cities RISE! has tested these principles and achieved remarkable success. I established RISE! to alleviate chronic poverty by enabling participants to get and keep a living-wage job with benefits. RISE! educates, trains, and places its graduates and then counsels them through the first year of employment. Its graduates do indeed get good jobs, and they keep them. From 2007 to 2010, their salaries averaged around twenty-five thousand dollars, about three and a half to five times higher than they earned before they entered the program, depending on the year.[1]

RISE! serves people who are among the most difficult to employ in our society, those who are underserved by other workforce programs. They are typically the product of generations of poverty and unemployment. Most are ex-convicts or single mothers living on welfare whose obstacles to employment include low academic achievement, homelessness, and drug and alcohol addictions. Over the past fifteen years, the one- and two-year job retention rates for participants who have graduated from RISE! have averaged 80 percent and 72 percent, respectively. These retention levels are higher than those our customers regularly report when hiring people who have fewer obstacles through more traditional hiring channels. Moreover, among the ex-felons who have graduated from our program, we have reduced recidivism by approximately 60 percent, improving their lives and the lives of their families and lowering the cost to society.

RISE! has demonstrated the power of these seven principles when applied to the nonprofit sector. The principles provide tools for effectively addressing social problems even while government spending on preventative social programs declines. And RISE! is just one of a new wave of organizations that are benefiting from putting these tools into action.

THE SOCIAL ENTERPRISE MOVEMENT:
NECESSITY IS THE MOTHER OF INNOVATION

Fortunately, as the need for more effective social organizations has become urgent, innovation is proliferating among organizations that have a social purpose. Throughout the world, entrepreneurs with a social agenda are experimenting with new business models, new ways to finance start-ups and growth, and new ways to combine the practices of business and charity. Social entrepreneurship has become a recognized global movement.

The term *social entrepreneur* was in its infancy in 1980 when the organization Ashoka was founded by Bill Drayton in Arlington, Virginia, to support such enterprises.[2] It took until 2006, when Muhammad Yunus, founder of Grameen Bank in Bangladesh, was awarded the Nobel Peace Prize, for social enterprise to achieve widespread recognition by the mainstream press, as well as by the government and business sectors.

Today the world abounds with pioneering organizations that have responded to the need for more productive social organization by finding innovative and successful ways to address social problems. They are getting these excellent results by using many of the same principles I present in this book. Throughout the book, I'll be focusing on these nonprofits and social enterprises that range over a vast continuum of size and scale, from well-established giants to younger, dynamic, and fast-growing organizations:[3]

- *CaringBridge.* Founded in 1997, CaringBridge provides free Web sites that connect people experiencing a significant health challenge to their friends, family, and other supporters. More than 275,000 Web sites have been created.

- *College Summit.* Founded in 1993 in Washington, D.C., College Summit has helped schools with low-income students increase their college enrollment rates by nearly 20 percent over what it was before implementation. College Summit works with 180 schools in twelve states.

- *Common Ground/Community Solutions.* Common Ground was founded in 1990 in New York City; Community Solutions, a spin-off, was launched in 2011. Common Ground works to end homelessness, particularly among the long-term homeless. It owns and manages housing that provides tenants with easy access to multiple support services. Community Solutions grew out of the work of Common Ground to bring proven innovations to communities seeking to end homelessness. Its national 100,000 Homes campaign seeks to get 100,000 homeless people into homes by July 2013.

- *Grameen Bank.* Formally established in a village in Bangladesh in 1983, Grameen Bank has grown to an institution that makes microloans to 8.32 million borrowers, 97 percent of them women, in 81,372 villages.

- *Habitat for Humanity.* Founded in 1976 in Americus, Georgia, Habitat's primary activity is financing and building, rehabilitating, repairing, or improving houses with volunteer labor, including sweat equity—that is, construction labor from the owners-to-be. The organization has approximately fifteen hundred U.S. affiliates and five hundred international affiliated organizations in nearly eighty countries, with combined total net assets of $2.1 billion.

- *Lumni.* Founded in 2002 in Chile, Lumni funds the higher education of students in the United States, Chile, Colombia, and Mexico. It raises capital from private investors and creates social investment funds that it manages in the expectation of making a profit. Rather than providing typical education loans, Lumni invests in students who commit to paying a fixed percentage of their income for a fixed number of months after graduation.

- *Playworks.* Founded in 1996 in Oakland, California, Playworks works to improve learning in low-income, urban elementary schools through safe, healthy, inclusive, and positive play. It provides schools with a trained adult who teaches games, conflict resolution, and leadership skills during recess and other designated times. As of September 2011, Playworks served 320 schools in twenty-one cities. Teachers report that with Playworks in their schools, they can spend significantly more time teaching and less time dealing with conflicts and other problems.

- *Twin Cities RISE!* Founded in Minneapolis, Minnesota, in 1994, Twin Cities RISE! seeks to end concentrated, multigenerational poverty by providing employers with skilled, reliable employees, primarily men of color. Since 1994, RISE! has grown from a pilot program with nineteen participants to an organization that serves more than fifteen hundred people every year.

These organizations are described in more detail in Appendix B and throughout the rest of this book.

The social enterprise movement is also demonstrating innovation in the funding of social ventures—new ways to capitalize on both start-up and growth. In 2009, Congress passed the Serve America Act, which includes provision for a social innovation fund. The fund enables the federal government to partner with the private sector in funding the scaling up of promising nonprofits that address our social problems.

Social entrepreneurs are testing new financial instruments that tap into the monetary value created when social ills are reduced. The social impact bond, launched in 2010, will fund programs to reduce recidivism among prisoners in Great Britain. In the United States, a group of colleagues and I have developed the human capital performance bond, a state-issued bond that will provide financing to social enterprises based on their achieving outcomes that increase state tax receipts (through higher incomes) and reduce state expenses (such as welfare and incarceration). A $10 million pilot has been approved by the state of Minnesota.

Social entrepreneurs have risen to the challenge of decreased governmental funding in this period of continuing social problems. Necessity has energized their power of innovation. Now is the time to accelerate these efforts.

HOW THE SEVEN PRINCIPLES WERE DEVELOPED

So how did I, an executive vice president of a Fortune 100 company, get into the poverty alleviation business and come up with principles for strengthening nonprofits?

It began in 1991 when I hit a wall. I was forty-five years old, jetting around the world and earning more money than I'd ever imagined. I liked the people I worked with. I was proud of my company. But I realized I wasn't growing or learning anymore.

I had begun working for General Mills in 1969, after earning my M.B.A. from the Wharton School at the University of Pennsylvania. Within eight years, I'd risen from marketing assistant to president of a new subsidiary, Yoplait USA. Within another six demanding but exhilarating years, we'd established Yoplait as one of the two dominant brands in yogurt. General Mills promoted me to executive vice president, to manage a group of domestic and international businesses.

At the same time, I was deeply involved with the community. I served on boards of for-profit and nonprofit organizations including the Donaldson Corporation, Minnesota Public Radio, the Bridge for Runaway Youth, and the Citizens League. Like other senior corporate officers, I served on the board of the General Mills's philanthropic foundation, where I had the opportunity to observe some great ideas at work and some things that provoked my thinking because they simply didn't make sense. The General Mills Foundation was considered at the time, and still is, one of the country's top corporate philanthropic foundations.[4] The company financed it consistently with about 3 percent of pretax profits and hired able leadership. General Mills supported a wide variety of social, educational, and cultural programs, including training programs for the poor. Our professional staff evaluated each organization and program thoroughly before recommending a grant. So it was clear that we wholeheartedly supported the training programs we funded, yet I observed that we rarely hired graduates of these programs. Why? For the most part, those graduates lacked the skills our company (and many other companies, too) required. My conclusion was that our standards for granting philanthropic support were lower than our standards for hiring people, a realization that provoked me to imagine better alternatives.

The General Mills Foundation also provided me with an unusual experience that demonstrated the strength of combining the best of business and nonprofit practices. I served as chair of ALTCARE, a joint program between General Mills and the Amherst W. Wilder Foundation, a large nonprofit in St. Paul, Minnesota. ALTCARE had developed a cost-effective alternative to nursing homes—a model for senior housing and assisted living that offered graduated health care as well as many of the amenities of homelike living, and at a substantially lower cost than a conventional nursing home. This joint project between Wilder, which knew senior housing and client care, and General Mills, which provided expertise in marketing and finance, was successful, and the model ultimately inspired the development of thousands of similar living arrangements for seniors throughout the United States. It convinced me that a combination of strengths from a nonprofit and a for-profit could tackle difficult problems and succeed.

In 1991, with a lot of ideas but no clear direction yet, I left General Mills and put my professional life on hold for a year. I vowed to spend more time with my family, especially my teenage son, Zack. With that vow, I headed directly to the personal and professional passion that would guide the rest of my life.

Zack was a member of the Minneapolis Initiative Against Racism, a group investigating poverty in the Twin Cities. At the invitation of Don Fraser, then mayor of Minneapolis, I joined the initiative's economic development subcommittee and began to immerse myself in the conditions faced by the poor. One afternoon the whole catastrophe suddenly hit me personally: What would I do if *I* were poor, black, and stuck doing menial work for low pay? How could I get a better job? Where could I go for help? Who would take a chance on me if I were a school dropout, an ex-convict, or a recovering addict—or some combination of these?

I set out to find the answers, and what I learned led me to found Twin Cities RISE! Since opening our doors in 1994, RISE! has grown from a pilot program with nineteen participants to an organization that serves more than fifteen hundred people every year.

Throughout my corporate and nonprofit experience, I had been identifying and practicing what makes organizations strong and successful. Founding RISE! forced me to articulate the principles I'd learned. In the early days, Michael Patton, who had professionally evaluated hundreds of poverty programs, counseled me, "Don't spend too much time on planning. Most organizations don't end up doing their plans as written anyway. Figure out the tenets you're going to live by and who you're going to serve. Imagine a couple of participants. What do they need? And how are you going to provide it?"

I based our initial principles on my observations regarding what I had seen work and fail in both sectors, as both an executive and a member of corporate and nonprofit boards. As RISE! grew, I revised them based on our experience. We've learned exciting and often humbling lessons about what works and what doesn't. I have talked with economists, researchers, and government officials and interviewed social entrepreneurs and the clients we serve. The seven principles in this book are the distillation of insight from a lot of good minds and lessons learned from the front line.

SEVEN FOR-PROFIT PRINCIPLES THAT BUILD NONPROFIT SUCCESS

So here they are, the seven principles. They first proved their worth in for-profit business. Now they've demonstrated that they can strengthen social-purpose organizations—nonprofits and for-profits alike—so that those organizations achieve long-term, sustainable results.

Principle #1: Have a Clear and Appropriate Purpose

Purpose establishes an organization's rationale for existence. It is what an organization strives to achieve, and once that purpose is established, it doesn't waver. It also expresses the passion that brings social entrepreneurs and nonprofit employees to their work. A clear and appropriate purpose inspires, guides, and energizes everyone associated with the organization.

Do you and those you work with believe, with every fiber of your being, that everyone deserves a decent place to live? Or a good education? Or the opportunity to raise themselves and their descendants out of poverty? Our purpose at RISE! is to reduce concentrated poverty, something we passionately believe in and work toward.

Your mission is what your organization does to fulfill its purpose. That is, the mission defines the aspect of the problem that your organization chooses to tackle and how you address it. For example, our purpose at RISE! is to reduce concentrated poverty, and our mission is to provide employers with skilled workers, primarily men of color who once lived in deep poverty. Our purpose drives not only our mission but also the way we measure progress and the way we communicate results. Great organizations refine their missions as they grow and learn and as conditions in the world change, but their purpose remains inviolate.

Principle #2: Measure What Counts

Metrics have a way of focusing our attention. Whether we're measuring return on investment or the SAT scores that colleges look at to determine admission, it's human nature to spend our time, energy, and material resources to improve that which is being measured. In a world of limited resources, it's critical to measure what counts because organizations get what they measure.

To achieve your mission, you have to focus on your desired outcomes—the results that fulfill your purpose. Getting a person off welfare and into a minimum-wage job may be an improvement, but does it significantly affect chronic, concentrated poverty? At RISE! we don't think so. So the outcome we focus on is the number of participants who get and keep a job that has an annual salary of at least twenty thousand dollars plus benefits for at least two years.

Many other nonprofits are pressured by government and other funders to focus on the inputs and outputs of their program rather than meaningful, long-term outcomes. For example, traditional job training nonprofits measure inputs (number of participants, number of courses taken, and number of hours in training, for example) and outputs (number of participants who graduate and the proportion who land a job). These metrics can offer useful information, but they are not outcomes. You can waste precious resources by investing them in improving input and output metrics unless those metrics lead directly to the desired outcomes.

Principle #3: Be Market Driven

There are many elements of marketing—advertising, brand management, and public relations, to name a few—but the most important one is the least often understood by traditional nonprofits: serving your customers. Again, it's a matter of focus. Every nonprofit has many important stakeholders with many and varied needs. But a market-driven organization recognizes only one group as the customer. Out of all your stakeholders, your customer is the one who, more than anyone else, determines your survival and success. And, interestingly, your customer is not necessarily the people you serve.

College Summit, for example, refers to the high school students that it's helping to get into college as its "clients." Understanding clients' needs and behaviors is a critical part of College Summit operations. But its customer is the school system and its representatives—the superintendent, principals, teachers, and other staff. The schools pay to bring in the program, although the amount is a small portion of the actual cost. The success of College Summit's mission is determined more by the commitment of these customers than anything else. College Summit is always thinking about what their student clients need, but when they determine priorities, the school and its staff come first.

Principle #4: Create Mutual Accountability

Successful organizations practice mutual accountability with every stakeholder, whether clients, participants, customers, donors, staff, or government. Mutual responsibilities are discussed up front, agreed on, and revisited as necessary throughout the relationship. When each party is held accountable for contributing to the venture, all parties are vested in its success, and the venture is more likely to be successful.

This is especially important for participants. When people get something for nothing, they don't value it. Mutual accountability ensures that participants value what they receive, which means they are more likely to fulfill their commitments and succeed in the long run. Accountability is a bedrock of a successful life.

For example, all Habitat for Humanity home owners help build houses—their own and usually someone else's—before they move into their own. Habitat believes that this principle of sweat equity creates a partnership with the home buyer. It believes that establishing mutual responsibility is not only the right thing to do for participants, but it builds community and attracts donations.

Principle #5: Support Personal Empowerment

Many organizations talk about empowerment as a feeling of self-confidence and optimism that people acquire in the course of participating in a program. At RISE! we've found that isn't enough. By *empowerment*, we mean a particular set of cognitive and emotional skills coupled with a positive belief system. Using these skills, a person can manage his or her emotions, thinking, and behavior to achieve positive, long-term life goals. Because of their positive beliefs about what is possible, empowered people don't sabotage themselves. Rather, they make choices that optimize potential benefits to themselves and society. Achieving this degree of empowerment requires significant training for our participants.

Like many of our nonprofit colleagues, we work with people whose families have lived in poverty for generations. Individuals who are raised in this culture of generational poverty frequently feel victimized, powerless, and entitled. As our participants grew up, they learned a whole set of beliefs, thoughts, feelings, and behaviors that enabled them to live in that culture—survival skills that have now become counterproductive because their old approach undermines their ability to achieve their current goals. RISE!'s empowerment curriculum is based on research from clinical psychology in two major areas: cognitive restructuring through cognitive behavioral therapy, a talking therapy that, among other things, teaches a goal-oriented system of techniques to help patients address problems of dysfunctional emotions, behaviors, and cognitions; and emotional intelligence, the ability to identify, assess, and manage the emotions of oneself, others, and groups.

Participants take empowerment training throughout the ten or more months they work with RISE! They take classes, receive individual support from a professional coach, and practice their empowerment skills within the culture of our organization.

For change to endure, people must transform themselves; they must stop feeling powerless and start taking responsibility for their actions, stop feeling hopeless about their future, and start seeing better possibilities within their grasp. We have found that the personal resiliency, perseverance, and positive sense of self that participants acquire through empowerment training is the most important factor in their success in the program, at work and in life.

Principle #6: Create Economic Value from Social Benefit

As a society, we are accustomed to thinking about social good in terms of moral imperative rather than economic benefit. But every improvement in social good does in fact have monetary value—to the participant, the state, or some other stakeholder. And in most situations, economists are able to assign a specific dollar value to that social benefit. Once we have that economic analysis, we can use it to develop new approaches to funding and financing social initiatives.

When a convicted felon gets a well-paying job and becomes a contributing member of society, obviously that's good. It's also economically valuable. When RISE! participants start earning a higher income, society benefits from increases in tax revenues and decreases in both public subsidies and the costs incurred by the criminal justice system.

We worked with economists to determine the precise numbers. This has made it possible to establish pay-for-performance relationships with the state and other funders. Our remuneration is based not on the number of participants we serve or even train, but rather on the number of graduates who get and keep a living-wage job with benefits, the value of which provides the state with an attractive return on its investment in RISE!

Recognizing the economic value of social good enables society to make better decisions about where to invest its limited resources and also allows the most successful organizations to grow.

Principle #7: Be Learning Driven

Great organizations aren't distinguished by getting it right the first time. Few, if any, do this. Rather, they are learning driven. That means you start your venture with a working model that makes sense based on your best thinking. Then you experiment, evaluate, adjust, experiment again, evaluate again, adjust again, and so on, until you achieve your outcomes. It takes a willingness to continuously gather intelligence about the environment in which you operate and regularly question your assumptions and practices. A learning-driven approach is an ongoing part of the strategy of great organizations.

Sometimes learning is imposed on us by outside forces like the 2009 worldwide economic recession or the 1998 flood that covered half the country of Bangladesh. Under crisis conditions, we are forced to find new ways to operate if we are to survive and continue working toward accomplishing our purpose. The recession led RISE! to create an internship program that proved to be so valuable we made it a permanent fixture in our program. The flood in Bangladesh pushed Grameen Bank toward several years of redesign that led to changes in processes and procedures so extensive that the bank is now referred to as Grameen Bank II.

The best organizations don't wait for a crisis. They incorporate learning into their daily operations. Everything we do at RISE! is subject to change if change can improve what we do. Being learning driven requires that we understand the shifting needs of our customers and other stakeholders, evaluate our processes and results, and consistently challenge the status quo.

WHAT TO EXPECT FROM THIS BOOK

This is not a scholarly work that attempts to present all that is known about building great nonprofits. It is my personal take on what I have learned—as a businessman, a nonprofit CEO, and a board member—about what enables organizations to excel. The seven principles are practical. They don't take sides when it comes to politics. The principles themselves are neither conservative nor liberal, neither Republican nor Democratic. They rest firmly on the social and economic bottom line. My hope is that understanding the power of these principles will benefit not only nonprofit practitioners but also those in the policy and foundation world who are making decisions about them.

I continue to search for better methods and better answers and to learn from the sharpest minds. In these pages, I present stories and examples not just about RISE! but other successful organizations as well. I interviewed some of the most dynamic and inspiring nonprofit leaders and social entrepreneurs of our day so they could tell you in their own words the lessons they've learned. They are extraordinary people—optimistic, bright, and very impatient.

Take Felipe Vergara. His for-profit social enterprise, Lumni, provides money for students in four countries to obtain postsecondary education. Lumni funds these efforts with private investment capital in an innovative system that has won international recognition. Years ago in graduate school, he heard Miguel Palacios, a researcher, talk about "human capital financing" and how it would probably be revolutionizing social enterprise financing in thirty years or so. Vergara's response was, "Why wait?"

He's right. Now is not the time to linger over how we did things in the past. It's time to harvest the best from the for-profit and nonprofit worlds and build organizations that are stronger than ever before. I invite you to put these seven principles to work in your organization and to insist that they be applied in the policies you support.

Why wait?

1

Principle #1

Have a Clear and Appropriate Purpose

Former Medtronic CEO Bill George likes to tell a story about an exceptional worker in his cardiac pacemaker factory. Her record of quality and speed stood out even in a group of high-performing peers. When asked what drove her, she replied, "I'm not making medical devices. I'm saving lives." Whether your business is pacemakers or yogurt or job training and placement, your workers need a reason to give their best to your enterprise. They need a reason to tolerate the inconveniences and obstacles that are part of daily work life. They need a clear and appropriate purpose.

I define *purpose* as why an organization was created, which is different from an organization's mission. Mission, what the organization intends to do to fulfill its purpose, speaks specifically to how this organization will bring value into the world. Purpose speaks to what that value is. Different organizations, including those referred to in this book, may use different terms for purpose and mission. The important thing isn't the specific terminology; it is the clarity with which your organization understands and practices these concepts.

This is true whether the organization is a nonprofit, a government agency, an artistic organization, or a for-profit corporation. Many people think that the main purpose of a for-profit company is to make money. I disagree. In my three decades of experience in the for-profit sector, I have observed that the best-performing organizations think of the bottom line as the result of focusing on purpose and mission, taking action based on that focus, and executing those actions well. They consider their profits an outcome rather than their reason for existence.

At General Mills, for example, some people would have said that Yoplait was in the business of manufacturing and selling yogurt. We recognized, however, that consumers wanted more nutritious, convenient, and great-tasting food. We saw ourselves as providing a delicious food choice that met their needs. As a purpose, that's not as earth-shaking as saving lives, but it provided a standard of excellence for our work that motivated employees and led to solid financial outcomes.

Why the emphasis on purpose in a book about social-purpose organizations? After all, organizations that tackle our greatest social problems already know why they exist. But the best organizations—whether for-profit or nonprofit—do more than know their purpose. They hold themselves accountable to serving that purpose in everything they do. They are more effective because they continually focus their efforts and resources on what will accomplish their purpose. They're less likely to get sidetracked. Too many organizations fall into the trap of being distracted from their original intent.

Here's how we might have strayed off course at RISE! Everyone knows that helping an unemployed person get a job is a good thing, so we could have been satisfied with getting any job for our participants. However, our purpose at RISE! is "to reduce concentrated poverty," so the bigger question is, Will this job raise this person out of poverty? Does placement equate to rising above poverty? Not if the job pays minimum wage and the person leaves after six months. A clear purpose not only sets direction, but functions as a standard against which to test all decisions and actions.

HOW RISE! DEVELOPED ITS PURPOSE AND MISSION

I founded RISE! in order to combat poverty in the Twin Cities. But before I could do that, I had to learn about poverty in the United States. I discovered that when Lyndon Johnson declared a war on poverty in 1964, about 20 percent of the total population of the United States was living in poverty, according to the U.S. Census.[1] The figure dropped steadily over the next decade to about 11 percent, due largely to the extension of social security benefits to the elderly. It bounced up during the 1980s, leveled off in 2006 to between 12 and 13 percent, and steadily climbed to 15.1 percent in 2010. By the same year, the rate of poverty among black Americans had also risen to 27.4 percent, more than three times the rate for whites, with much higher figures among younger black men.[2]

After three decades of spending federal and private money on this issue, why had it grown worse and not better? I decided to find out.

In 1993, I visited antipoverty and job training programs in Minneapolis, St. Paul, Chicago, Indianapolis, Atlanta, Detroit, Los Angeles, and New York. I met with scores of people who were committed to guiding the poor toward economic self-sufficiency. I found a continuum of processes and results among the providers. At one end of the continuum were hundreds of nonprofits that provided short-term training and placement services for the poor. Their goal was to get people into jobs—any jobs. Typically these jobs paid minimum wage or just above it. These nonprofits were financed primarily by federal Jobs Partnership Training Act programs for poor adults or by welfare-to-work programs directed toward parents, who were almost always unmarried women.[3]

Most of these programs operated on the assumption that once people got started on the path to economic self-sufficiency, they could bootstrap themselves the rest of the way.[4] I found no evidence to support this conclusion in evaluations of federal programs.[5] In addition, little government support existed for programs that aimed to provide jobs that pay a living wage[6] (about twenty thousand dollars annually, plus benefits) to people with multiple barriers to success like a criminal record, low academic skills, few occupational skills, or drug and alcohol abuse.[7]

At the other end of the continuum of antipoverty program providers were community colleges, technical and trade schools, and proprietary education programs. Although they often enroll people with multiple barriers to success, the graduation rate is low: fewer than 15 percent of them earn degrees.[8] Without the skills to secure better-paying jobs and with limited access to training that would increase their job skills, these disadvantaged workers remain stuck in dead-end jobs where real earnings—as well as employment levels—have been decreasing since the 1970s.

At the same time I was researching antipoverty programs, I sometimes heard people who were not working with the poor say things like, "My father came to this country with nothing, and he made it to the middle class. Why can't they?" Underlying this statement is the question: Why do some of our American poor remain stuck in poverty while many immigrants are able to work their way up? The answer lies in the distinction between situational and generational poverty.[9]

Those whose poverty is related to their situation—being an immigrant or having lost a job or a spouse—have been impoverished by circumstances. They often succeed in overcoming their poverty as a result of help from family support, skills acquired in previous jobs, and personal qualities like a strong work ethic. They believe that if they work hard and make sacrifices today, their tomorrows—or their children's tomorrows—will be brighter.

The prospects are quite different for some groups of poor Americans, when two or more generations have lived in poverty. A culture can emerge that typically produces a damaged sense of self-worth combined with a feeling of entitlement: *I'm a powerless victim. Someone else is responsible for my situation and owes me.* Most harmful of all is the sense of hopelessness that accompanies this mind-set: *If there's no hope, why take action?* But those who don't take determined action to rise above poverty won't do so.

In developing our purpose and mission, it became clear that we had to address generational poverty and come up with something that produces better results than those that existed at the time.

RISE!'S PURPOSE AND MISSION
—AND HOW THEY HELP US SUCCEED

At RISE! we put a lot of time and energy into deciding what our purpose and our mission should be. The effort paid off by making us more effective at achieving our outcomes.

We define our purpose as reducing concentrated poverty and our mission as providing employers with skilled workers, primarily men of color who were once poverty stricken. Our purpose focuses on concentrated poverty. Generational poverty thrives in concentrated, economically depressed, mostly urban neighborhoods. This concentrated poverty is less amenable to change and more damaging to our society than poverty in general. Children who are raised in such an environment of high unemployment, high crime, housing decay, and hopelessness have a hard time escaping poverty. Therefore, improvements in concentrated poverty have the potential to bring great benefits.

Our mission focuses on employers as our customers because employers supply the jobs. They set the standards for

---

RISE!'s Purpose and Mission

Purpose: To reduce concentrated poverty

Mission: To provide employers with skilled workers, primarily men of color the job market in which we place individuals. Our success or failure as an organization depends on our ability to meet their needs. Our mission also focuses on job training for men of color, although we enroll people of both sexes and all races. Why? Impoverished minorities have represented an increasing proportion of the Twin Cities population—4 to 8 percent in the 1980s when we were developing RISE!, a number that was projected to double in each of the next two decades.[10] In addition, the Twin Cities have the dubious distinction of having an unusually high gap in unemployment rates between blacks and whites.[11] In 2010, according to the U.S. Bureau of Labor and Statistics, it was the worst in the nation.[12] Impoverished men are underserved because programs designed to get people off welfare serve custodial parents who are primarily women. At the same time, these men have great potential to help their families break the cycle of generational poverty by becoming role models and contributing to the family income as resident parents or through child support payments, to name just a few ways. Federal and state policy (and spending) doesn't squarely address the great leverage that these men can have in reducing the long-standing poverty of these families.

Because we are dedicated to breaking the cycle of poverty, we target jobs that start above the poverty line—jobs that pay no less than twenty thousand dollars a year plus benefits. In addition, our training is geared toward preparing our graduates to succeed at jobs that not only pay a living wage but provide benefits and offer prospects for advancement. In other words, RISE! is not a quick fix for the problems of poverty. We're committed to long-term solutions. Training that enables a person to obtain a job but not keep it and grow doesn't serve the interests of that individual or society.

Consciousness of our purpose reinforces our long-term perspective. The world is always changing; this includes the types of skills and employees needed, the kinds of participants who come to us at RISE!, the requirements of funders, and the economic and political climate. When something does change, focusing on our purpose enables us to adjust our course without losing our sense of direction.

A clearly defined mission operationalizes an organization's purpose. It says, "Here's what we do," and, by implication, "Here's what we don't do." A clear mission helps ensure that people have clear goals and don't get sidetracked, wasting valuable resources in the process. The success of any organization depends on using that mission to guide your actions.

In our early days, for example, we considered operating a facility to house men in the program who were homeless, since a lack of safe and secure housing is a primary reason for dropping out of the program prematurely. Our research revealed that operating a housing facility would require additional capital, risks, and skills that we didn't possess. It also identified other competent organizations already providing these services, and so we decided that operating such a facility wasn't central to our mission. Furthermore, we could address the problem by developing relationships with independent housing providers, which we did. As a result, we remained focused on the areas where we had skills and were building a competitive advantage while avoiding a direction that would have diverted our attention and resources.

THE ALL-IMPORTANT ALIGNMENT
OF PURPOSE, MISSION, AND PROGRAMS

When purpose guides mission and mission determines programming, you have a beneficial chain that makes any enterprise, business or social, more effective. With the organization headed in a clear direction, people make better decisions and use resources more wisely. The organization is more productive.

In the case of RISE! our mission states that we serve employers by providing skilled workers, so our programming must meet employers' needs. To develop our curriculum, we solicit input from employers as well as from adult education experts and other human development experts.

Based on that input, we provide extensive training and development to prepare participants for jobs in two primary areas: operations (materials handling, warehousing, manufacturing, and machine operations) and office support (customer service, clerical work, financial services, and call centers). That training covers not only occupational skills but also remedial academic subjects, such as computer training, math, reading, speaking, and writing.

To accomplish our purpose and mission, we have discovered, we also must provide training in personal accountability and empowerment, two of the proven principles that are essential for success in the world of work. Including this training separates our approach from virtually all other poverty and training programs.

A new cycle of classes begins every ten weeks. On average, the program takes thirteen months to complete, although some participants take less than six months and others up to two years to graduate. The difference depends on what competencies and barriers they enter with and what obstacles arise along the way. For example, some have had to drop out to attend to family emergencies and have returned later.

Our purpose gives us a long-term perspective, so our program reflects that. Unlike many other programs, our commitment is not time dependent. In exchange for participants' dedication, hard work, and mastery, we guarantee that we will work with them as long as it takes—whatever they need to develop marketable skills, use those skills to get a job, and stay on the job for at least one year. As long as a person is showing up on time, doing the work, and moving toward full employment, we continue to invest in him or her. Our program is designed to prepare participants for their long-term commitment to their new jobs and more productive lives.

WHEN MISSION MET REALITY AT COMMON GROUND

An organization's purpose is a steady and unwavering statement of its intention. Its mission and strategies, however, may need to change—or be rethought—as it encounters a world that behaves differently from what its leaders anticipated. Common Ground's purpose is and always has been to "end homelessness," but when its original mission and strategies hit a stumbling block, the organization managed to rethink and alter its approach.

One of its first triumphs occurred in the early 1990s when it finished converting the historic Times Square Hotel in New York City into 652 supportive housing apartments for tenants who were low income, formerly homeless, or living with HIV/AIDS, or some combination of these. Supportive housing incorporates services that address tenants' mental and physical health issues, helps them pursue jobs and education, and otherwise moves them toward stable and productive lives.

Common Ground saw its role in ending homelessness as providing exemplary housing for the people it thinks of as "the most vulnerable among us." It had what founder and president Rosanne Haggerty calls "a housing mission."

Then came the great letdown—and the great aha!—that moved Common Ground from focusing solely on developing housing to ultimately creating a national organization to spearhead today's 100,000 Homes campaign.

"We started out as housing developers," says Haggerty. "Our innovation was doing supportive housing at a much larger scale [than had been done before], serving a mixed-income group, incorporating job creation and training." She continues:

> After we'd done the Times Square project, we continued
> to see the same people on the street who lived there
> before we did the project. This wasn't supposed to
> happen. We wondered why we hadn't reached them.
> Outreach teams working with the homeless on the street
> told us that these individuals refused their help and were
> choosing to be homeless. We foolishly believed that.
>
> [Then one day] we got a call from a local hospital. An
> elderly woman had named us as her next of kin and
> wanted to move to the Times Square Hotel. She turned
> out to be one of the people we'd seen on the street for

years. We broke all our rules and found a way to move her right away into the building.

When she moved in, we asked her why she hadn't wanted to move into our building before. And she told us, "Nobody asked me. People asked me if I wanted to go to a shelter or stay on the street. Nobody ever asked me if I wanted help finding my own place."

That was the great aha! We then sent two interns out to talk to the people living on the street. We were stunned by what we learned. No one had been offered help with housing. What these individuals wanted was a home; they didn't want to be in shelters because they felt frightened or dehumanized there. Yet there was no system to connect them with anything but shelter.

That was the beginning of what became the "Street to Home Program," a process for moving the most vulnerable homeless directly into homes and systematically reducing street homelessness. We learned that you have to ask a lot more questions and look at people's actual experience of homelessness. In fact, for most people who are homeless, it's a very short-term experience and they find their own way out of it. We learned that we needed to focus on those who got stuck in homelessness and help them through the process of finding a home. That was a revelation to us and the field.

Common Ground's purpose—to end homelessness—was as strong as ever. But what it had learned led it to refine its mission. To have greater impact on the problem as a whole, Common Ground began to prioritize its efforts toward the long-term homeless. But who were these people who spent years, and even decades, living on urban streets?

Haggerty and her colleagues became familiar with the public health work of James O'Connell and Stephen Hwang, physicians who had studied the causes of death among homeless people. People living on the street often die young—in their forties and fifties—from a combination of physical and mental problems. They do get medical care in emergency rooms, but that's expensive, and continuing care is a problem. Most have nowhere safe to store their medications, no refrigerator to preserve insulin or other drugs, and often limited ability to get to follow-up visits with a physician.

"If you want to solve a public health problem, you have to figure out who's most vulnerable, to understand degrees of severity," says Haggerty. "We realized that a public health approach should be applied to homelessness, and to begin to solve this problem we needed to know who specifically was in the worst health. And to use housing as a critical intervention." With O'Connell, Hwang, and other collaborators, Common Ground developed a "vulnerability index" that ranks the homeless by health risk and prioritizes them for housing.

Common Ground still develops and manages supportive housing, because, notes Haggerty, "There is still a shortage of affordable and supportive housing." Tenants succeed in their buildings, which have a retention rate of between 85 and 90 percent.

But, Haggerty continues, "it's been very interesting. In the first twenty years, with our housing-focused mission, we assisted over forty-five hundred people in overcoming homelessness. But we knew that truly working to end homelessness would require a new way of working, which is why Community

Solutions was formed. In the past eighteen months, we have organized partners throughout the country to adopt the tools and processes that reduce street homelessness." In July 2010, Community Solutions launched the 100,000 Homes campaign, a partnership of organizations in more than ninety communities working collectively to place 100,000 of the most vulnerable, chronically homeless people into permanent supportive housing by 2013. As of July 2011, over 10,000 had been housed, on track to meet that deadline. Clearly introducing a new strategy and organization to focus first on the homeless person and then on the housing appears promising.

All nonprofits can learn from the Common Ground/ Community Solutions experience. You hold steady to your purpose. But just as important, you need to maintain flexibility when it comes to mission, strategy, and tactics. Common Ground kept expanding its understanding of the problem it was addressing and the environment it operated in. It used that knowledge to adjust its mission, strategy, and tactics and even to spin off a new organization to become more effective, by an order of magnitude, at serving their purpose.

COMMUNICATING YOUR PURPOSE TO EACH GROUP OF STAKEHOLDERS

The purpose and mission of an organization must be communicated clearly, frequently, and in specific ways to each stakeholder. Why take the trouble to convey this message to all stakeholders rather than just customers or participants? Stakeholders who clearly understand your purpose and mission are better able to support it. They give you better feedback on the effectiveness of your efforts. They are more willing to work through difficulties. You are able to develop a stronger, long-term relationship with your stakeholders, and they become partners in serving your purpose as a result.

Communicating purpose and mission is an essential and ongoing task that requires understanding the perceptions and misperceptions that each group is likely to have—and the ways in which they receive information best.

Nonprofits take on big challenges. We can use all the help we can get. Hone your message to the needs of each group of stakeholders. Find ways to reinforce that message on an ongoing basis. When you need stakeholder support, they will know why you're important, they'll believe in you, and they'll be there.

Here's how we hone and communicate our message at RISE!

Participants

To help participants understand our mission, we reinforce it from the first day of their probationary period in the program through to the end of their first year of employment. Mission finds its way into every written communication: our handbook, written agreement with participants, and training materials. We design our physical environment to be as businesslike as possible to communicate the professional approach that our mission implies. Teachers, trainers, and coaches convey the message in personal and group communications. (Coaches are staff members who teach, mentor, and troubleshoot, working one-on-one with participants to help them succeed at RISE! and in their first job after graduation.)

We hold a celebration every ten weeks where we recognize participants' accomplishments in achieving our mission. We present a ring to each graduate who has been on the job for one year. These celebrations also help our staff and volunteers to recharge their batteries and renew their sense of accomplishment and purpose.

The media we use to communicate with our other stakeholders are fairly typical—personal meetings, e-mail blasts, annual reports, quarterly letters. But we tailor our message carefully—to address each group's understanding and possible misunderstanding.

Customer Companies

To help customer companies, we have found that we need to address confusion about the business approach we take toward alleviating poverty. For those who think of RISE! as a job training and placement organization alone, we clarify that we are an antipoverty organization. We help our customer companies understand that we view training and placement as solutions for alleviating poverty—our reason for being. This does not mean, however, that our standards for skilled employees are compromised by our purpose. A key part of alleviating poverty is to provide fully qualified employees who keep their jobs and progress in their work lives.

Contributors and Funders

We help contributors and funders understand our purpose and mission—especially those who challenge our focus on training men of color. Our message to contributors is that we do accept all races, genders, and ethnicities; however, our priority is on men of color because of the enormous leverage they can have in alleviating generational poverty. As responsible wage-earning men in communities where children know few such men, they can be powerful role models. They also provide income toward raising their children, which can lift a family above the poverty line, something a single parent working at minimum wage often can't accomplish. And they are under-served by both private and government-sponsored programs because of the governmental focus on reducing welfare rather than alleviating poverty.

Staff

To help our staff understand our purpose and mission, we give them ongoing opportunities to encounter them. We have company meetings where our purpose and mission are explained, discussed, and sometimes challenged. Both are prominent in our employee handbook. Most important, we operationalize purpose and mission through our programming, and we articulate to employees how we have done so.

At RISE! I speak with every new employee. I want them to understand our mission and principles intellectually, of course. But I also want them to experience the passion with which our organization was founded. This communication process is particularly important because each person brings different expectations and experiences from his or her background in social services, business, or education.

STAYING FINANCIALLY SECURE
WHILE HOLDING TRUE TO YOUR MISSION

Maintaining the integrity of your mission can be quite a challenge when funders are providing funds for initiatives that are related to your mission but really don't support it. Some nonprofits chase such monetary support because they believe it's the only way they can survive. That's a bad idea, but it's tempting.

When I spoke to Felipe Vergara, cofounder of Lumni, which funds higher education costs through private capital, he had just completed a round of funding and was aware of how difficult staying true to your mission can be. Vergara explained, "When you are beginning an organization, there is a tyranny in the scarcity of cash. The principles are in the mind and the heart of the leader. But you need to pay salaries at the end of the month. Cash difficulties are a huge distortion sometimes."[13]

The key is to avoid offering a jumble of unrelated programs that reflect the interests of your funding sources rather than your own purpose and mission. Organizations that get too far off course never reach the critical mass that enables them to make a difference in any one area. They ultimately lose sight of their purpose. This is why so many organizations don't do as much good as they might and why some close down.

At RISE! maintaining the integrity of our mission proved to be more challenging than we anticipated. Millions of federal dollars were readily available for welfare-to-work initiatives, short-term training, and working with higher-functioning dislocated workers, but much less was (and is) available for longer-term training for people with criminal records, low skill levels, and multiple personal issues. I'll admit we were tempted to go after the easier money—though in the end we didn't because that would have meant not being true to our mission. This isn't to say that supplementary ventures inevitably subvert an organization's purpose. Many nonprofits successfully generate funds from leveraging their intellectual property.

As a board member of American Public Media/Minnesota Public Radio, I was privileged to participate in one of the best of these ventures—a highly successful, revenue-producing initiative that began accidentally. Founded in 1967, Minnesota Public Radio (MPR; and its parent company, American Public Media) began as a single classical music radio station and has grown into the largest regional public radio network in the country: a forty-two-station network serving virtually all of Minnesota, parts of surrounding states, and stations in Los Angeles and Miami. It also syndicates nationally shows that it produces, like *Marketplace*, *Speaking of Faith*, and *A Prairie Home Companion*. With an impressive list of awards, it has grown into an influential national presence.

One of the reasons for MPR's remarkable growth has been its ability to convert its know-how into money-raising ventures that have generated support for its mission-driven activities. MPR's purpose (which it calls its mission) is "to enrich the mind and nourish the spirit, thereby assisting our audiences to enhance their lives, expand perspectives and strengthen their communities." It does this by creating and broadcasting news, entertainment, and music programming. In the process, it creates a great deal of intellectual property, including the program that first brought it national attention, *A Prairie Home Companion*, a radio variety show hosted by Garrison Keillor that is broadcast in the United Sates and internationally by public radio stations and the Internet.

In the early days of *A Prairie Home Companion*, long before it became a national hit, Keillor promised during a broadcast to send a Powdermilk Biscuit poster to anyone who asked for one. (Powdermilk Biscuits is a fictional sponsor of the program, and its catchy little jingle is sung during every show.) I suspect MPR was testing how many listeners were paying close attention. Expecting only a handful of requests, the show's staff was overwhelmed, and dismayed, when thousands of requests poured in. To fulfill all of the requests could have meant financial ruin for the station. Thinking quickly, MPR decided to honor every request and, in hopes of defraying the cost, to include with each poster an order form for T-shirts, coffee mugs, and other *Prairie Home* paraphernalia.

Again, the response far exceeded expectations. It had to develop a major mail order business to meet the demand—a wonderful thing that ultimately led to even more problems. The revenue from selling the merchandise not only threatened the station's tax-exempt status as a nonprofit, it also overwhelmed the governance capabilities of its board. So MPR's parent organization formed Rivertown Trading Company and its holding company, Greenspring Corporation, a separate, for-profit corporation with its own board to oversee the station's business enterprises. Some members of the board were common to both organizations to ensure MPR's interests were served, but the majority of directors were chosen for their business acumen alone. This enabled the MPR board to focus on its mission and purpose while its for-profit board focused on running a business. I was a member of both. No longer were MPR board meetings concerned with inventory risks, for example, a subject better left to its for-profit. Over the years, Greenspring (through its Rivertown Trading Company subsidiary) provided tens of millions of dollars to MPR for its operating and capital needs. MPR later sold Rivertown Trading for more than $120 million and used the money to boost its endowment and to fund additional projects.

So by using business ingenuity and leveraging its intellectual property, MPR was able to stay true to its mission, finance its growth, and remain financially secure. MPR has become the most successful and largest regional public radio organization in the country, as well as a pioneer in Internet media.

I looked for ways in which we at RISE! could also leverage our intellectual property. It was clear that the empowerment program we had developed could be valuable to others in the business, nonprofit, and education worlds. Such a venture would offset the costs of running our core program and increase our base of customer contacts. And the more feedback we received from these other groups, the more we could improve the training.

I was convinced that we could market our empowerment curriculum without getting sidetracked from our purpose. Our board had its doubts. Some members thought that the effort would divert resources and management attention from our primary objectives. Others were concerned that it would require investment spending we couldn't afford. Still others worried about a potential conflict for resources. For these good reasons, we decided to start small. We created the Empowerment Institute, a specific group within RISE! that is managed separately so that RISE! can focus on its mission. The Empowerment Institute earns revenue to support RISE!'s mission by marketing our empowerment training to customers in markets outside those RISE! is dedicated to serving. Institute staff conduct training and also do train-the-trainer sessions using a curriculum we designed to take our content to participants outside our program. Our first customers were in the corporate and social services sectors, and we continue to work with clients there. More recently we've been working in education. Colleges and universities have an acute need to improve retention and graduation rates, especially among students who are the first generation of their family to attend. Our empowerment training is helping students deal with stress and continue their education while improving the educational institution's revenue (since students who continue their studies continue to pay tuition). In public middle schools, our empowerment training is giving students with behavior and emotional disorders the skills to attend mainstream classes. Corrections programs are using our empowerment training to improve reentry and recidivism among former convicts. The list of empowerment applications goes on and on. (You'll read more about the Empowerment Institute in Chapter Five.)

As we hoped, the Empowerment Institute has increased our revenues and extended our contacts for our core business. It has also served to confirm the value of our empowered approach to solving difficult issues in schools, universities, prisons, and other organizations. Seeking new sources of revenue by exploiting intellectual capital is often tempting, and it can certainly be a worthwhile venture that contributes to financial stability. However, you need to be careful to organize, resource, and govern these activities so that they do not interfere with your purpose and mission. Otherwise you risk jeopardizing your organization's very reason for being.

A SENSE OF PURPOSE
IS ESSENTIAL FOR HUMAN SURVIVAL

How important is purpose, really? Many of us have worked in places where purpose is just an inspirational slogan on the wall that people rarely even glance at. Is that really so bad? If we step out of the realm of organization life and into one of the darkest times of world history, we learn that human beings need purpose. It's as elemental as food or water. A wise leader respects that human need and responds to it.

I find great insight in the work of Victor Frankl, a Holocaust survivor. In his book *Man's Search for Meaning*, Frankl contemplates what made survivors of concentration camps like himself different from many of those who perished under Nazi barbarism.[14] It wasn't physical strength, age, or even health that determined who lived or died, the distinguished Austrian psychiatrist wrote. Many who were weaker, older, and sickly survived when others did not. Frankl concluded that survivors were distinguished by their ability to envision a future for themselves despite their suffering. They believed there was purpose to their lives then and in the future. They did not surrender to despair.

It may seem counterintuitive for an older person to be able to envision a future better than a younger one, but that is exactly the point. People of all ages and conditions can choose to live a life dedicated to purpose. The survivors were literally living proof of Friedrich Nietzsche's maxim, "He who has a why to live for can bear any how."[15]

Most of us will never go through anything like the horror that Frankl experienced, but the lesson is clear: as people and organizations go through triumphs and tragedies, they are more likely to thrive if they are focused on a clear and appropriate purpose.

For exemplary organizations, mission and strategy, and goals and tactics, are open to adjustment based on changing conditions and ongoing learning. Purpose is not. It is the guiding force and moral compass that keeps us focused on our true north. It is inviolate.

QUESTIONS TO HELP YOUR ORGANIZATION BECOME MORE PURPOSE DRIVEN

- Does your organization have a clearly articulated purpose that motivates people to do their best?
- Does your mission articulate specifically how your organization serves your purpose?
- How do you communicate your purpose and mission? Exactly what do you say, and where do you say it? What do you communicate with your behavior? (Your actions are more important than anything that you hang on the wall or put in an employee handbook.)
- What are the specific barriers to communication for each group of stakeholders? How could you tailor the message— and the way you communicate that message—to best reach each group?

- Are the services or products you provide in alignment with your purpose and mission? Is there some enterprise or activity that doesn't fit but nonetheless has become part of your organization's work? This could be the result of legacy decisions, financial reasons, decisions made in crisis mode, or deliberate, well-thought-out choices. Are the reasons currently compelling enough to continue pursuing that activity, or are you diverting precious resources that could be spent on achieving your mission?

- Should you adjust your organization's approach to serving your purpose in light of new information or changing circumstances? Could you become more effective by shifting your focus, as Common Ground did? How has your understanding of the issues you address become more clear and accurate? What actions does this suggest?

2

Principle #2

Measure What Counts

There is no lack of measurement in the nonprofit world. When I was doing my due diligence before forming RISE! I saw existing programs dedicated to poverty reduction making great efforts to get accurate numbers. These organizations knew how many people they were serving, how many units of service they were providing, and how many people completed their programs compared to how many had started. They knew how many they placed in a job immediately after leaving their program.

They worked hard to improve these numbers, and many did, year after year. But they rarely followed up a year or two down the road. They didn't know how their participants were faring out in the real world. Therefore, they really didn't know how effective they were in reducing long-term poverty. And the funders who supplied them with financial support didn't know how good an investment they were making.

These nonprofits were staffed by good, hard-working people, but in my opinion, they weren't measuring what counts. This is one reason our nation has been more successful at getting people off welfare than we have been at reducing chronic poverty.

You get what you measure because metrics have a way of focusing people's attention. It's human nature to put our efforts into achieving whatever we will be measured on. And that's fine, as long as those metrics have been carefully chosen to get us to what's really important. If not, we can end up scoring high on the metric but not achieving our purpose.

Lessons in the for-profit world abound. Let's say a large company is starting a new business within it. If corporate salespeople are rewarded simply on units sold, they will tend to sell whatever is easiest to sell—which is probably not the new business's products. So you may get excellent revenue from your sales team and good short-term profits, but you've inadvertently contributed to the failure of your new business. You have to focus on the results you want and develop metrics that will support those results. Good sales strategies target not only the volume but the mix of products the company wants sold, and then they provide incentives for achieving those results by setting minimum quotas for each type of product or providing better rewards for the products that are tough to sell.

When a for-profit organization discusses results, the metrics are usually clear and explicitly stated. Industries use common financial measurements such as earnings-per-share growth, unit sales growth, and return on assets. The fact that these measurements are used consistently makes it possible for investors to evaluate a company's performance and compare it to others they may be considering investing in. It also allows managers to evaluate their own performance and make adjustments to strategy and the effective deployment of resources.

Measuring success in the world of nonprofits is, to put it mildly, less uniform. My review of a wide variety of social service programs in the antipoverty, job training, health care, education, and other fields showed no generally accepted industry-wide measures of success or any consistent methodology for measuring outcomes.

Some people who wish to donate to charity—the nonprofit equivalent of for-profit investors—have traditionally used ratings supplied by Charity Navigator, the American Institute of Philanthropy, and similar organizations. This is one attempt at developing common metrics for all nonprofits. These ratings help donors compare the worthiness of nonprofits as potential recipients. A typical key metric is the proportion of funds spent on services versus administration and fundraising costs. Although this figure is useful, it doesn't measure how effective the organization is at accomplishing its purpose.

If you want to accomplish your purpose and mission, you have to measure the extent to which you are accomplishing that. You have to measure your outcomes—your actual results. And measuring outcomes requires understanding the critical distinctions among inputs, outputs, and outcomes.

THE DIFFERENCE IN MEASURING INPUTS, OUTPUTS, AND OUTCOMES

Inputs and outputs refer to what goes into and comes out of a process. In the case of social-purpose organizations, the process in question is your process for creating social change—in other words, your program. Traditional job training programs tend to measure inputs like the number of participants and hours of training provided, and outputs like classes completed, cost per individual served, and number of graduates. There is nothing wrong with measuring inputs and outputs. Indeed they can be essential milestones on the way to achieving your mission. But they are not outcomes.

Outcomes are your results—serious indicators that you are creating the long-term social change that your organization is dedicated to. You define your desired outcomes based on your knowledge of what contributes to your purpose, a dose of common sense, and what is feasible to measure. In establishing your target outcome, you may also find it useful to think about what does not work as an indicator that you are achieving your mission and purpose. For example, we know that getting a minimum-wage job for a single parent with four kids doesn't raise that family out of poverty. And we know that an ex-felon working on a job for two months and then being fired for a bad attitude hasn't been raised out of poverty either. These negatives can help us establish what does work. Choose an outcomes metric that makes sense and is practical to measure. At RISE! we chose getting and keeping a living-wage job with benefits for at least two years.

Relying on outputs as if they were outcomes can lead to bad decision making, inappropriate allocation of resources, and ineffective organizations. The reason is that when you invest resources in improving your outputs, you may or may not be making progress toward achieving your mission. You just don't know.

A traditional job training program, like those described at the beginning of the chapter, may be investing in strategies and tactics that reach the output of placement but do little to ensure the longer-term success of that placement. Placement is a necessary metric but hardly sufficient. To understand their outcomes, job training programs should be measuring the change in income from the training, retention in the job, and return on investment to various stakeholders, including government and philanthropy.

Managers of the best for-profits do measure the inputs and outputs of internal processes—like cost per item, quality, inventory turnover, and sales volume. All of these are important, but only insofar as they contribute to the ultimate outcome, the bottom line. Good managers know how the metrics work in relationship to one another and what leverage points will prove most valuable in achieving desired outcomes.

It only makes sense to hold people accountable for behavior that is within their span of control—salespeople for sales numbers rather than inventory turnover, for example. But when you choose a metric, you are choosing how you plan to spend your human and financial capital. You need a good idea of how that metric will affect other metrics and how it affects your outcomes. You can determine that only if you are actually measuring outcomes.

One of management's chief functions is to decide how to allocate the organization's resources in a changing world. In an economic downturn, can we serve the same number of people as before? We certainly want to continue working toward our purpose with the same intensity. And, after all, if we admit the same number of people to the program, our input numbers will stay at the same level. But if we can't provide each person with the support and training we've found to be essential or if there are fewer jobs to be had, our outcome numbers will suffer. Worse yet, if the organization goes under because it doesn't live within its means, we won't be able to serve anyone at all.

Weighing the trade-offs between financial realities and purpose is an ongoing part of the job. To make informed choices, managers need metrics that truly express outcomes.

In these days of reduced budgets, those who fund nonprofits—philanthropists, foundations, and government—are becoming more sophisticated about allocating their resources to achieve the best results. These funders and policy thinkers are asking fundamental questions about the differences among inputs, outputs, and outcomes. They are advancing new incentive systems for public and private service providers that reward true outcomes over mere outputs. In the future, social organizations that don't focus on outcomes are likely to be left behind as a world with fewer resources demands more accountability of measurement and outcomes.

GRAMEEN BANK: CLEARLY DEFINING THE OUTCOME

Measuring outcomes accurately requires first defining those outcomes precisely. Grameen Bank provides a stellar example of how we can use precise metrics to describe a beneficial condition: the outcome "out of poverty."

Grameen Bank's founder, Muhammad Yunus, received the Nobel Prize for, among other things, his pioneering work in microlending to the very poor in Bangladesh. The obvious metrics for a lending institution are number of borrowers, size of loans, rate of repayment, and other profitability indicators. Grameen does in fact measure all these things. Its Web site offers quite a bit of financial data, just as you'd expect from a bank founded by an economics professor. But the most important outcome that Grameen is seeking to improve is "the socioeconomic situation" of its members—to help them move out of poverty. To that end, Grameen had to decide precisely what it meant by "out of poverty." It did so by developing a definition, the Ten Indicators:[1]

> A member is considered to have moved out of poverty if her [almost all Grameen members are women] family fulfills the following criteria:
>
> 1. The family lives in a house worth at least Tk. 25,000 [about $350] or a house with a tin roof, and each member of the family is able to sleep on a bed instead of on the floor.
> 2. Family members drink pure water out of tube-wells, boiled water or water purified by using alum, arsenic-free purifying tablets or pitcher filters.
> 3. All children in the family over six years of age are going to school or finished primary school.
> 4. Minimum weekly loan installment of the borrower is Tk. 200 [approx. $2.81] or more.
> 5. Family uses sanitary latrine.
> 6. Family members have adequate clothing for everyday use, warm clothing for winter, such as shawls, sweaters, blankets, etc., and mosquito-nets to protect themselves from mosquitoes.

7. Family has sources of additional income, such as vegetable garden, fruit-bearing trees, etc., so that they are able to fall back on these sources of income when they need additional money.

8. The borrower maintains an average annual balance of Tk. 5,000 [$70] in her savings accounts.

9. Family experiences no difficulty in having three square meals a day throughout the year, i.e., no member of the family goes hungry any time of the year.

10. Family can take care of [its] health. If any member of the family falls ill, family can afford to take all necessary steps to seek adequate healthcare.

In addition to defining specific outcomes for each member, Grameen defines specific outcomes for each branch:

1. Borrowers repay 100% of their loans.
2. The branch is profitable.
3. Deposits are greater than outstanding loans.
4. All children of each member are in school or have completed at least primary school (one of the ten indicators).
5. All members have crossed over the poverty line (as defined by the ten indicators).[2]

Every Grameen branch is evaluated on a five-star system in which a star of a particular color is awarded for the achievement of each of the five goals.

The first three outcomes reflect the financial health of the branch: 100 percent repayment by members, the branch's profitability, and deposits greater than outstanding loans. A financially healthy branch is important to members because it survives to make loans in the future and because members are shareholders: 95 percent of the equity in the bank is owned by borrowers. The remaining two stars proclaim achievements in rising out of poverty: one star for all children in school or having completed at least primary school and a second for all members having crossed over the poverty line.

Obviously the branch's outcomes are connected, but not precisely correlated, to the ten indicators—education is so important that it receives a separate star. But this system of outcomes works for Grameen, and that's what's important. Outcomes data were not yet available for the whole system, but Grameen states that members and staff derive motivation, energy, and direction from their respective sets of goals—for crossing out of poverty or becoming a five-star branch.

WHY ORGANIZATIONS DON'T MEASURE OUTCOMES

If outcomes measurement is so great, why don't more organizations do it? Overworked leaders of nonprofits can be heard wailing about one of these two excuses:

Excuse 1: "But the funders require input and output data."
Excuse 2: "We can't afford it! That kind of project takes money away from our services and those we serve."

Excuse 1 is quite true. Funders such as philanthropies and government agencies often require input and output numbers because they are tooled up to make decisions based on process rather than results. In addition, politicians are often influenced by the two-year election cycle to demonstrate quick results (outputs) rather than meaningful outcomes that take longer to materialize and then measure and evaluate. So you have to accept reality and collect data that may or may not be important to you, but are certainly important to the people who are important to your organization.

Excuse 2 is true only in a very shortsighted way. Inputs and outputs are easier, cheaper, and faster to obtain than outcomes. But in a world of limited resources, you need to know if your organization's way of doing things is working. If you don't measure outcomes, you don't know how well your resources are being invested. Outcomes measurement isn't another layer of expense added onto your budget; it's a necessary cost of operations because it provides managers with the information to make good decisions about what works and what to improve.

The investment in outcomes measurement is one of the significant differences between for-profit organizations and nonprofits. Well-run for-profits are always seeking to refine their strategies and tactics to optimize the return on investment from their resources. They ask questions like these:

- How is the marketplace changing?
- What are our competitors doing?
- Can investment in a new process improve quality or lower costs—or both?

- Will increased advertising expense or lowering prices increase share of market, unit sales, and ultimate profitability?

Making accurate strategic decisions requires investment in information about operations and the marketplace. It is not inexpensive, but without it, companies would suboptimize, much as many nonprofits do. Investing judiciously in intelligence is the only way to know whether you are optimizing your resource allocation and, ultimately, your outcomes.

In addition, government, philanthropies, and foundations are becoming increasingly interested in outcomes. Providing them with outcomes data can be a crucial factor in differentiating your results from those of other organizations and in obtaining financial support. In some cases, philanthropies and foundations may even be a source of funding for measuring outcomes and establishing the economic value these outcomes provide. But whether you receive additional support or not, obtaining intelligence that leads to better results and measuring outcomes is fundamental to your ability to succeed. Not doing so is penny wise and pound foolish.

WHAT GOOD OUTCOMES MEASUREMENT LOOKS LIKE

To measure outcomes, we need metrics that meet two critical criteria:

1. They measure the organization's ability to deliver against its purpose and mission.

2. Stakeholders recognize them as obvious, clear, relevant indicators of achievement (or lack of it).

At RISE! we measure results by asking these questions:

- How many individuals did we place in jobs that pay at least twenty thousand dollars per year plus health benefits?

- How many stayed in those jobs for more than one year?

- How many stayed in those jobs for more than two years?

- How much did their income increase as a result of their RISE! training?

- How much was recidivism reduced for participants with previous felony convictions?

- What is the return on investment to our state government investor?

These are the answers to those questions as of this writing in 2011:

- Over the past fifteen years, one-year and two-year retention in jobs to our graduates has averaged 81 percent and 72 percent, respectively.

- The average income increase of graduates has been approximately fifteen thousand dollars. We have measured recidivism reduction of former felons since 2005. For graduates, it represents a 66 percent reduction.

- The return on investment to the state of Minnesota since 1997 stands at 624 percent, or $7.24 for each dollar that the state has invested.

We also evaluate more traditional data such as the number of people served, the number who complete classes, and the number who were placed in jobs earning less than twenty thousand dollars per year. But we don't use those data to determine our bottom-line success.

If measuring outcomes means long-term follow-up, as it does in our case, how far out do you go? Ideally you should follow people until they have stabilized, which might be two years or five or ten. Or you would evaluate the changes in generational poverty over several generations. A few multimillion-dollar medical studies do in fact take such a long-term approach. But the rest of us have to consider what's feasible. We have to think about what's reasonable in terms of our purpose and in terms of cost. Tracking Americans over long periods of time becomes increasingly difficult and costly as they move on with their lives. So at RISE! we've settled on two years as a time frame that makes sense. During those two years, we stay actively in touch with our participants and their employers. That way we are immediately aware of any problems that come up, which is useful knowledge for us, and we can help resolve those problems.

In the future, we hope to obtain aggregate data based on tracking the social security numbers of groups of participants, provided that government will cooperate. Aggregate data will provide us with information about the whole cohort, not a particular individual. Individual privacy would be protected and the information we received would allow us to evaluate programming and return on investment over a longer period of time. The use of aggregate data that the government collects by tracking individuals opens up the possibility of measuring the effectiveness—the true outcomes—of various social interventions by nonprofits.

Although such aggregate data are not yet always readily available, nonprofits can still go a long way to improve outcomes data. Of course, we can do only what's feasible and practical. Such data are well worth the resources that we need to obtain them, as long as you and your stakeholders agree that these indicators truly measure your organization's ability to deliver against your purpose and mission.[3]

THE DANGER OF APPLES-TO-ORANGES COMPARISONS

It's important to keep in mind that not every organization is committed to measuring true outcomes—yet. The stakeholders you report to—government and other funders—may be receiving a confusing mixture of input, output, and outcomes data. It's easy for them to draw erroneous conclusions, so it's your responsibility to clarify the situation.

When I started RISE! in 1994, few nonprofits were reporting outcomes because few foundation program officers or government officials required them. The result was that it was difficult to explain our outcome results without being compared (unfavorably) with another organization's output results. They'd ask, "How come you have fewer graduates than they do?" or, "Why are your costs per placement higher than theirs?" I'd explain that RISE! was reporting how many individuals obtain and keep a job above twenty thousand dollars with benefits, an outcome that would truly lift participants out of poverty. The other organization's cost per placement—in any job, at any salary, with few if any benefits—was an output. Their number of graduates was an output. But I still received a lot of blank stares. More than once, this confusion between outcomes and outputs affected whether we received financial support. It also led to funders misrepresenting our results.

I came up with a useful analogy to clarify this difference. Reporting how many individuals got any job at any salary would be as if General Mills reported to its stockholders how much wheat it processed (an output), when they are justifiably interested in how many boxes of Wheaties it sold (an outcome). Stakeholders found this helpful, but it didn't clear up the problem entirely.

Some of our staff became so concerned that they suggested we drop reporting our outcomes and instead report the output standards of the industry. If we had done so, it would have made a mockery of our purpose. We would have taken our eye off the ultimate goal for which our organization was founded and would have risked settling for lower performance. In response to the reality of industry measurement and evaluation practices, we chose to report our outputs along with our outcomes so that a more familiar context could be provided to those evaluators while keeping our principle intact.

This strategy of providing outputs as well as outcomes data works well. It enables people to see numbers they are comfortable with, while providing the opportunity to explain the critical importance of outcomes. It also conveys how an outcomes-focused nonprofit is distinguished from other organizations the stakeholder may be considering funding.

We have learned that it takes a long time to change industry practices, but it is also important to stay the course.

MOVING TOWARD THE FUTURE IN MEASUREMENT

Measuring what counts gives social-purpose organizations power. When legislators and other funders ask, "So what?" we have the answers. We can provide numbers that reflect the long-term benefits our efforts have for participants and society. Those numbers enable them to answer to their constituents and stakeholders. With outcomes data, we can begin to establish the economic value of the benefits we provide. We can establish pay-for-performance systems that fund our growth and so bring our benefits to more people who need them. If it's true that you get what you measure, let's measure the right stuff and get the benefits.

QUESTIONS TO HELP YOUR ORGANIZATION MEASURE WHAT COUNTS

- Do you measure outcomes that truly reflect how well you are achieving your purpose and mission?
- Are your current metrics inputs, outputs, or outcomes? Inputs and outputs can be very useful in evaluating day-to-day operations and satisfying some stakeholders, but they aren't

effective for determining whether you are achieving your purpose and your mission.

- Do stakeholders recognize your outcomes metrics as obvious, clear, and relevant indicators of achievement (or lack of it)?

- What would you like to measure but think you can't? What's the barrier? Is it too complicated, too expensive? What's the benefit? What would it take to implement? Think creatively. Maybe it's more possible than it seems.

3

Principle #3

Be Market Driven

When I speak to groups about RISE!, I tell the audience that we regard employers as our customer, our only customer, although we serve many stakeholders. I emphasize that paying attention to our customers' needs is the most important part of being a market-driven organization, which is what we strive to be. This statement always provokes questions: Why employers? Why not participants? Why think in terms of customers at all? Why this focus on the market and who you're marketing to? "After all," their argument goes, "you're a social services nonprofit. You're not a business that relies on the market to earn a profit."

Then I tell them about Willie Sutton, the infamous bank robber. Asked once why he robbed banks, Sutton reportedly answered, "Because that's where the money is." Employers are our customers because that's where the jobs are. Employers are our market.

If our programs don't meet employers' needs, participants won't meet those needs and they won't be hired or, if they're hired, they won't be retained. Although we don't rely on the market to make a profit, we certainly rely on it to meet our goals and achieve our mission—as do all other nonprofits, whether they realize it or not.

Marketing encompasses many elements—advertising, brand management, public relations, and pricing, to name a few—but the most important one is often the least understood by traditional nonprofits: serving your customers. Again, it's a matter of focus. Every nonprofit has many important stakeholders with many and varied needs. But a market-driven organization recognizes only one group as the customer. Out of all your stakeholders, your customer is the one who—more than anyone else—determines your survival and success. Interestingly, your customer is not necessarily the people you serve.

Yes, nonprofit organizations have a social purpose and a mission. But we nonprofits operate in a market-defined world just as for-profits do. To accomplish our missions, it's essential that we know who our customer is.

Some people question whether being market-driven sullies an otherwise commendable social services mission. But the two worlds do not and should not operate independently. Just as the best for-profit organizations succeed because they have worthwhile and strongly articulated purposes, the most successful nonprofits understand their markets and tailor their strategies accordingly.

Some nonprofits don't see the world in this way. Their antipathy, even hostility, to this view has hindered their ability to fulfill their social missions. Unfortunately these nonprofits generally fail for the same reason that many for-profits fail: they don't identify their customers correctly. Nonprofits sometimes believe that their customers are their clients, the government, their funders, and other groups, but they are confusing their customer with all their other stakeholders. This is not to say that other stakeholders are unimportant. They are much like stakeholders in a for-profit business whose needs require attention as well. But our ability to meet the needs of the customer dictates success for all stakeholders. A job training program that cannot place and retain graduates in jobs that employers want filled is not serving its clients, funders, or any other stakeholder well. Having more than one kind of customer makes it too difficult to focus on the real drivers of success. It disperses resources over too many objectives.

Your commitment to being market driven should dictate everything you do, from how you are organized and governed to how you design your program, to where you are located, and those you hire. Success requires employing the best ideas from the nonprofit and for-profit worlds.

IDENTIFYING THE CUSTOMER AT CARINGBRIDGE

CaringBridge is a nonprofit organization that provides a place on the Internet where people who are going through cancer, difficult pregnancies, or other serious health issues can easily establish a Web site to keep in touch with friends and family. Its stated purpose is "to amplify the love, hope and compassion in the world, making each health journey easier." The employees of CaringBridge rarely, if ever, see the sites' users, but the company does conduct a great deal of research on them. To help employees hone the services they offer to the needs of particular users, CaringBridge has created user "personas"— for example:

- "Patty Patient," who typically journals and is the primary recipient of the community's support

- "Abby Author," the Web site developer (who is often not the patient but his or her primary caretaker)

- "Violet Visitor" and "Vince Visitor," who read Abby and Patty's updates and post their messages of support

- "Donna Donor," who has experience with CaringBridge and is planning to make a small cash donation in honor of his or her loved one

Profiles of each of these personas are posted on a corridor wall in the office for all to see. They are detailed, covering everything from the biography (age, occupation, hobbies, and household income), to technology use (How old is the home computer? Do they use the texting feature on their cell phone?), to needs and goals. For example, Abby Author is Patty's sister. She's forty-seven years old, with a husband and two children at home and is a manager at a small company. Violet Visitor is Patty's niece. She's twenty-eight years old, single, and with an entry-level white-collar job at a large corporation.

But who is the customer? CaringBridge's purpose is "to make each health journey easier." Patty and Abby, as the patient and the primary caretaker, respectively, are the most involved in the health journey and are the primary recipients of the love, hope, and compassion the purpose seeks to amplify. They are the equivalent of another organization's "participants." Clearly they're extremely important. But so are Violet, Vince, and Donna (not to mention various foundations and hospitals whose support is critical to CaringBridge).

CaringBridge's mission (which it refers to as its goals) is this:

- Ensure families receive the love and compassion they need during a significant health challenge.

- Reach out and serve more families.

- Enable financial gifts, volunteering and in-kind donations from donors and volunteers.

Founder Sona Mehring says, "We talk about the 'community of family and friends coming together when they need it most to provide love and support.' Over the years we've said that Abby and Patty are our primary customers and Violet and Vince Visitor are secondary. Now [after talking with you] I'm wondering if we have that reversed."[1]

What difference does it make? If CaringBridge identifies Violet and Vince as their customers, will it still do outreach to hospitals and other sources to reach Abby and Patty? Of course. But customer definition prioritizes the strategic use of resources. If Violet and Vince are the customers, their needs are paramount. And in the case of CaringBridge, that means that the development of mobile apps moves way up on the list of priorities. More and more, Violet and Vince are using smart phones. And CaringBridge has found that many people communicate with their telephones in a more personal way than they do with the computer on their desk. The CaringBridge site that Abby creates still has to be easy to use and look good on a home computer screen. But the same site now has to work well on a handheld device—both visually and on the technological platforms of those devices.

Patty Patient and Abby Author are certainly the primary users and beneficiaries of CaringBridge's services. CaringBridge was founded to make their lives better. But that doesn't make them the customer. More and more, Mehring says, she is realizing that the people who determine CaringBridge's success are the community of support, that is, the site's visitors, Violet and Vince. When it comes time to budget funds to serve the needs of stakeholders, the needs of customers come first.

THE MARKET IS ALWAYS CHANGING: LISTEN AND BE FLEXIBLE

Most markets are in a constant state of change. It's up to you to adapt, whether that means redefining your customer, your strategies, your tactics, or even your mission. Your market may be changing technologically, as it has for CaringBridge with increased use of smart phones, or because of world events, as it did for RISE!

In our case, we had always known that certain companies would not hire ex-felons for regulatory, safety, or fiduciary reasons. Nevertheless, we had been successful in placing ex-felons in a few top-notch companies. Then, after September 11, 2001, companies became more risk averse. They hired risk managers who convinced them to reduce their risk profile. To some businesses, that included eliminating interviews with ex-felons and in some cases even misdemeanants. In addition, the slowing economy created a shrinking market for labor, with experienced, overqualified professionals often willing to take jobs for less pay. We began having a serious problem placing graduates in white-collar jobs like customer service and administration with some of our existing customers.

We eventually understood that the hiring climate had changed for the long term, and because more than 70 percent of the men at RISE! were ex-felons, this market shift had a significant impact on our program. We responded by adding a track to our training program that prepared participants for blue-collar jobs such as materials handling and machine operation. Our sales team began courting smaller companies that didn't have the same prohibitions against hiring ex-cons that many large companies do.

The results were dramatic. By 2006, almost half of our graduates had landed jobs in the blue-collar arena at yearly wages exceeding our minimum standard of twenty thousand dollars, plus health benefits. Also, our number of customer companies grew substantially, to more than fifty per year.

By remaining flexible, we made the necessary changes to our program while staying on course with our mission. We recognized changing priorities in the market's needs. We became better equipped to provide training and placement opportunities for participants with difficult criminal pasts, a group we are committed to serving.

Being flexible and adapting to new market needs is vital. Successful organizations are constantly refining their product mix, introducing new services, and changing their marketing approach as they work to meet the needs of a changing market.

HOW A MARKET-DRIVEN APPROACH
PLAYS OUT AT PLAYWORKS

Jill Vialet, president of Playworks, is passionate about helping low-income kids. Her vision is that every child in America will be able to play every day. And if you think that's a frivolous goal, she'll point you to the data on the childhood obesity epidemic, studies that show how physical activity increases academic performance, and the research that has established how many hours of classroom time teachers don't spend teaching but dealing instead with conflicts and bullying issues that arise during recess and lunch time.[2] You can hear the warmth in her voice when she talks about providing "coaches" to low-income schools—how the coach creates recess that is fun, provides healthy exercise, and sends students back to class ready to learn.

Vialet founded her enterprise, as most other social entrepreneurs do, because of how deeply she cares about her cause and her participants. But she's a hard-headed marketer when it comes to her relationship with customers. She knows who her customers are and how to serve their needs, an understanding has served the organization well:

> I care about what we do—on a cellular level—because of
> the benefits that I see that play brings the kids—and how
> it changes their understanding of learning, gets them
> physically active, and is ultimately an incredible
> springboard for seeing themselves as change makers.
>
> But when I go into a potential school to talk with the
> principal about purchasing our services, I don't talk to
> them about any of those things. I talk to them about the

fact that Playworks is a cost-effective solution to their
group management problem at lunch and recess. Because
that really hits them where they're being accountable.
That's the value and that's what they're purchasing. We're
very market driven and I'm pretty clear that the principals
are my market.

Vialet understands that her purpose is about helping her
participants, but to accomplish that purpose and mission, the
organization needs to be market driven: it needs to recognize
the importance of the customer and know the difference
between participants and customers.

Being market driven also establishes credibility with donors
and investors. The relationship that nonprofits have with these
funding organizations is another major success factor, and they
are becoming increasingly savvy and demanding. They realize
that social-purpose organizations are not just social providers
but also organizations that need to make sense financially.
They are asking many of the same questions that for-profit
investors ask: What are your funding sources? Who are your
customers? What are your results? How will you sustain
yourself?

A few years ago, Playworks received funding from the
Robert Woods Johnson Foundation to expand its programs
from 115 schools in five cities to 700 schools in twenty-seven
cities. This funding initiative is similar to what venture capital
frequently does with for-profit companies when they finance
"taking the model to scale." One factor in the investment is
Playworks' market-driven focus on customers and its sophisticated approach to pricing its service of providing a trained
and supervised coach to low-income schools.

It costs Playworks between forty-eight thousand dollars and sixty-five thousand dollars to place a coach in a school for a year, but it charges each school about half of that. As sophisticated marketers, its leaders don't give away their services, because customers tend to undervalue what they receive for free. They don't use a cost-plus approach (cost plus profit margin, a common pricing strategy) because their customers can't afford it. Playworks has assessed the value of its services to customers and developed a model that works: it charges each school about twenty-five thousand dollars and supplements the rest through philanthropy. Says Vialet:

> We've done a pretty good analysis of what the market can bear. Twenty-five thousand dollars is about what schools can shell out on their own. Principals will universally say, "It's hard to come up with that much money." And yet they still feel they're getting an incredible deal at twenty-five thousand dollars with our program.
>
> That investment by the schools has been absolutely critical to our success. It ensures that the schools have skin in the game. They take the program seriously, value it, have high expectations, make accommodations that reflect the value of the program to them. That changes how it's implemented and received. It affords us a greater chance of success.
>
> Second, a principal who has invested twenty-five thousand dollars in a program has high expectations, and that enables us to manage more remotely. One program manager can oversee eight schools. We know that if a principal is unhappy with the quality of service they get,

they will be on the phone very quickly to complain. And that really works for us.

And third, there's the benefit with funders: "The fact that a low-income school has come up with twenty-five thousand dollars is easily leveraged because funders hear nothing but the fact that schools are broke. So if they're coming up with twenty-five thousand dollars, it reflects the value of the program."

Playworks' market-driven approach keeps the organization healthy and produces results that directly benefit its purpose: "To improve the health and well-being of children by increasing opportunities for physical activity and safe, meaningful play." David Bornstein, a reporter for the *New York Times*, interviewed several principals who use Playworks at their schools.[3] These principal-customers reported that their playgrounds went from places where a quarter or a third of children were active, to safer environments where 80 to 90 percent of students chose to involve themselves in games. Playground injuries and discipline problems had dropped by an order of magnitude.

Vialet refers to the financial benefits that schools receive as well. Schools think in terms of "recaptured teaching time"— the time their teachers now spend teaching instead of solving problems that originated in the playground. According to Playworks, many schools recapture more than thirty-six hours of teaching time, which schools value at $100,000 or more.[4]

Playworks' market-driven approach and focus on the customer pays off for everyone involved. Schools get to focus more on learning and less on discipline. Teachers get to spend more time teaching. And kids get to enjoy the benefits that play can bring to their physical and mental well-being.

CUSTOMERS MAKE THE BEST ADVISORS AND AMBASSADORS

Listen to your customers. They'll give you the best information you can get about your market. This may seem axiomatic, but a surprising number of organizations don't have systems in place to take advantage of their customers' knowledge and connections. You should because your customers will spot trends early. They can give you feedback on your programming. They know other customers and can help get you in the door to present your offering. The best way to ensure that you're listening to your customers is by making them part of your team.

RISE!'s board of directors is made up principally of employers because of their know-how about the marketplace and human resource issues, as well as their ability to influence hiring at their own and other companies. Supplementing the board at RISE! is our Employer Advisory Group, made up of human resource professionals and hiring managers from our customer companies. This group has been invaluable in defining the changes in work skills that employers seek. For example, during the "jobless economic recovery" that occurred after the slowdown as a result of the terrorist attacks on September 11, 2001, it was especially useful having so much market intelligence on tap. During this period, employers became less interested in people who had specific work skills and more interested in people who were flexible and, when given additional employer-sponsored training, could perform a variety of very different tasks. Without close relationships with our customers, we would have been in serious trouble: we would have been using old job descriptions when employers were instead seeking people with new skills. Therefore, we were able to shift our curriculum and prepare participants to do what employers needed.

During a time of great change, we needed great advisors, and our customers were already in place—on the board and in the advisory group—helping us remain relevant to the marketplace.

MARKETING MEANS LEARNING THE CUSTOMER'S CULTURE

At General Mills, I headed our international business. Executives at any successful global company will tell you that you cannot market the same way in every country. A strategy that appeals to Americans might seem crass to the French and offensive to the Japanese. Every market has its culture; its ways of doing things; language, dress, and behavior that are desirable; and language, dress, and behavior that should be avoided at all costs if you want to accomplish your objectives.

So when I became president of Yoplait USA, I studied French. My goal was to become bicultural—to learn enough about the language and culture to build productive relationships with French business executives.

To do business in a culture that's different from yours and to be effective, you have to learn your customers' culture. Then, to whatever extent is reasonable, you adapt to the local customs. You practice the language and the behavior.

It's sound business strategy, and it applies to different cultures within the same country as well. Any nonprofit that is marketing its services to another culture would do well to learn everything it can about that culture and practice adapting to it.

RISE! participants are products of the culture of generational urban poverty—with its unique set of customs, dress, and language. The culture of our potential employers is as different to some participants as the culture of a foreign country would be. Since our mission is to place participants in good jobs in the business world, we've found it invaluable to adopt many of that world's practices as our own. At RISE! we know that to succeed in the world of work, people need to know the culture of business—its rules, its language, its behavior—so we make it a point to familiarize our participants with those rules and to begin acquainting them with that environment. We chose a management structure that reflects the structure of our customer companies. We have a president/CEO and a chief operating officer rather than an executive director and a programming manager. We know that executives talk to other executives. Our management structure enables us to develop contacts at a high level in the employer organization so we can cut through red tape and get a leg up on job placement.

To help participants make the transition to the workplace, we designed our offices to accustom them to their future surroundings. When participants walk in our front door, they enter a business environment, not the environment of a training facility, school, or social services program. They are greeted in a friendly and professional manner. Respectful communication is strictly enforced: no loud talking, excessive socializing, or cell phone or iPod use. Dress is business casual.

Displayed to the left of our receptionist's desk are the names and logos of employers who have hired from us over the years. To the right, and on the walls leading to our classrooms, hang many portraits of RISE! graduates, with their company affiliations beneath their photos. We designed our entry in this way to remind participants of what they are here to achieve. We are communicating that RISE! is about enabling them to get the skills they need to achieve a living-wage job with upward mobility and work for employers like the ones they see in those photographs.

Our policies also mirror those followed by our customer-employers. Our program catalogue, much like a college handbook, describes our courses, career paths, and skill outcome requirements. It also extensively covers our policies for professional conduct, dress, and Internet use, as well as our strict prohibition of drugs, alcohol, and weapons.

We test for drugs because most of our customers do, not because many of our participants have a history of alcohol or drug abuse. Drug testing is part of the customers' culture. Besides, it would be pointless to invest in participants only to have them fail a test later that prevents their ultimate employment. We remind participants that they will be given a random drug test sometime during their first four weeks in the program. Despite the warning, a surprising number fail, most commonly because of marijuana. Since we practice the principle of accountability, we require them to leave the program immediately. If they are clean two months later, we invite them back. Some people just need to find out for themselves if we're serious about our policies. We are. So are our customer-employers.

If your participants will be expected to live or work in an unfamiliar culture, they need more than skills training. To be successful, all participants must also be able to function well within the written and unwritten rules of the culture they are about to enter. It's your job to see that they are prepared.

MISPERCEPTIONS CAN CHALLENGE A MARKET-DRIVEN APPROACH

Ironically, some of our for-profit customers have had difficulty understanding us as a marketing-driven nonprofit. Their previous experiences with nonprofits—as charities seeking a grant—affect their ability to comprehend our intention to be a supplier of quality labor. Other customers were haunted by the generally poor experiences they had had with other non-profits that supplied them with underqualified labor.

Perceptions like these can lead to false assumptions and misunderstandings—like the wrong people showing up at a meeting or the right people with the wrong agenda in mind. It's up to you to anticipate these possibilities and be absolutely clear. If you're doing business in a way that is new to them, you need to teach them how to work with you and demonstrate the benefits that they receive when they do business with a market-driven nonprofit.

At more than one initial meeting, I have been greeted by people from the customer's philanthropic organization, even though I'd arranged to meet with the human resource personnel. When this happened, we politely but firmly explained our approach and asked to meet with those who could hire our skilled workers.

We also found that some employers had lowered their hiring standards to meet the charitable need of putting unemployed people to work. This is a bad idea. These employers had failed to consider the consequences to those employees if they failed to keep their jobs, or the consequences to their company when new employees couldn't or wouldn't perform adequately.

An internal challenge we faced was the temptation to fundraise with companies that we were approaching to become customers. After all, we'd done the due diligence required to understand the company and we'd begun to develop relationships with key people. But we found that such a strategy is likely to confuse company personnel, and it's up to us to clearly establish from the start our role as a market-driven enterprise that provides skilled workers to customer companies.

We have found it best to avoid asking any corporate foundation for philanthropic support until after we have established a solid working relationship with its operating units. Once we are known as a reliable supplier of skilled labor, we aren't bashful about requesting donations. This relationship is not unlike some university affiliations with businesses, where they work under contract as suppliers and also enjoy philanthropic support.

If you are a market-driven enterprise, the customer relationship with customer companies has to be the most important relationship you have with them. Be clear on the nature of that relationship within your organization, and then express it clearly through words and actions to those outside your walls.

BY SERVING ITS CUSTOMERS, A MARKET-DRIVEN NONPROFIT SERVES EVERY STAKEHOLDER

The most important factor affecting a nonprofit's ability to serve its participants is its ability to meet customer needs. When the customer is accurately identified, the nonprofit puts its resources where they will do the most good. When the nonprofit has systems in place to listen to its customers and respond, it spots changing trends in the market before they become problems. When a nonprofit understands the customer's culture, it can deliver its service or product better. When the nonprofit is focused on customer needs, its operations are more efficient and results improve.

A market-driven, customer-driven nonprofit is more effective in achieving its social mission. At the end of the day, all stakeholders—customers, participants, the community, government, and philanthropic organizations—are better served.

QUESTIONS TO HELP YOUR ORGANIZATION BECOME MORE MARKET DRIVEN

- Who is your customer? Think about all your stakeholders: all the groups that influence you in accomplishing your mission, all the groups whose needs you take into consideration in your work, and all the groups that you benefit. Which group's behavior is critical to achieving your specific outcomes? Which one establishes the market standard for your organization's success?

- Do you—or the people you work with—have an aversion to being market driven? How do you feel about taking the best practices from both the for-profit and nonprofit sectors to fulfill your mission?

- How can you tap into the knowledge and experience of your customers to help your organization succeed? Do you include them in an advisory group or on your board of directors? Do you connect with them at senior levels as well as at the level where transactions are done?

- Given the characteristics of your market, how can you best interact with your customers to accomplish your mission? Create a portrait of your customers: their goals, needs, and situation in the world. How can you best meet those needs?

- What do your customers tell you about how their needs are changing? What do they tell you with their behavior rather than with their words?

- How should your strategy change in response to the market information your customers give you about the changing marketplace? What's going to continue to work well? What used to work but is becoming less effective?

- How should your organization's culture reflect the culture of your customers? Think about language, behavior, curriculum, rules, physical environment, and reward systems.

4

Principle #4

Create Mutual Accountability

Accountability, the bedrock of a successful life, is the most fundamental of the seven principles and should affect every organization at every level. It should guide the way you deal with every customer and every stakeholder.

Politicians and philanthropists, pundits and the public, for-profits and nonprofits all demand accountability. But the critical factor that they sometimes forget is this: accountability is a matter of mutual responsibility and shared commitments among all parties in the transaction. Accountability starts with the belief that if you give something to someone at no cost to him or her, this person will not value it. Value, in the corporate world, is primarily determined by the give-and-take of the market. When businesspeople are given something for nothing, they tend to be suspicious. However, if you ask for payment or some service in return, they quickly determine its value to them. If the recipient doesn't want to pay the asking price, the supplier must either adjust it or lose the sale.

Too much public policy in the United States has tried to help people out of poverty by giving them something for nothing. But when people get something for nothing often enough, the things they receive lose their value. They come to believe that everything can be had for nothing and begin to act as though they have a right to whatever comes their way without making any effort of their own. Entitlements may help people survive, but long-term use doesn't lead people to become independent. Accountability does.

Common Ground is an organization that understands the importance of shared commitments and responsibility. That's why it requires everyone who lives in Common Ground housing to pay rent. "Supportive housing is a situation of mutual accountability," says founder Rosanne Haggerty. Whether residents are formerly homeless or lower-income working people, "they're not there as program participants. They are tenants, with the rights and responsibilities of a lessee." Rent is 30 percent of a tenant's income. They're expected to pay on time and be good neighbors. In return, they can expect Common Ground to provide them with well-managed housing and access to the support services they need.

Tenants benefit because these responsibilities force them to practice essential behaviors they need to become independent, hold a job, and conduct healthy relationships. Common Ground benefits financially from tenants paying rent, although the payments don't come close to covering costs. In addition, by engaging with tenants on terms of mutual accountability, Common Ground establishes a foundation for sound financial and social contracts in all the areas in which it does business.

HOW RISE! PRACTICES ACCOUNTABILITY WITH ALL ITS STAKEHOLDERS

From the start, the RISE! staff affirmed that we would create value by requiring reciprocal accountability from all of our stakeholders. For services rendered, each participant, each staff member, and each customer-employer, as well as the government, has to give something in return. Most important, we expect participants to stay the course, finish what they start, and, ultimately, keep a job. If they aren't accountable in the program—if, for example, they're always late, don't do their work, or frequently don't show up—we put them on probation: they need to meet specific requirements to remain. Failing that, we ask them to leave for a period of time until they are ready to recommit. We are strict about accountability because the world they aspire to requires it. If they're not accountable on the job, they're going to lose it. If they are accountable, they're more likely to be retained and promoted.

The relationship between participant and coach is the most important factor in teaching accountability at RISE! All participants are assigned a RISE! coach—an advisor, teacher, mentor, and troubleshooter—to guide them through their time in the RISE! program and for the first year or so of employment. In some cases, the relationship lasts for over three years, including program and on-the-job time.

Participant and coach create a mutually agreed-on plan for the participant's tasks and classes for each ten-week session. At the end of that period, the two of them review the plan, evaluate progress, and create a plan for the next ten weeks. Like an athletic coach, a RISE! coach boosts morale or assigns consequences as needed. The coach meets with other staff to evaluate the participant's progress and determine next steps in the participant's development. Through language and action, the coach reinforces the lessons of empowerment and accountability. Coaches help participants develop problem-solving skills so they can solve their own problems (rather than solving problems for them). Coaches also refer participants to outside resources they may need, like housing or legal help. Finally, once the participant is employed, the coach works with both employer and employee as needed to ensure a successful placement.

The coach's most important role is to teach the accountability we expect from participants. We believe this strongly: accountability is a participant's path to success, and ours as well.

The Participant Agreement: Making Accountability Clear and Concrete

For any system of accountability to be effective, expectations must be clear. No one can be held accountable if they aren't clear on what the standards are. This is why at RISE! we make sure all of our participants understand what is expected of them.

Most people who come to RISE! have their own ideas about what the program is, regardless of what we tell them upfront. They want a job. They want a better job. They want to get out of poverty. And most of them want it today, not tomorrow. For much of our society, especially the poor, immediate gratification is the only gratification that seems real. But RISE! doesn't deliver immediate gratification. On average, participants take thirteen months of hard work to graduate from RISE! Some take longer. So we must reframe their expectations.

To make the principle of mutual accountability clear and concrete, we emphasize and reemphasize it in writing, recruitment conversations, orientation sessions, and one-on-one staff interviews with participants. We also use a formal participant agreement. It states that RISE! agrees to provide participants with high-quality training and job placement services at our expense. In turn, participants pledge to complete their training, take a living-wage job that we will help them secure, and perform well at that job.

Before a participant signs the agreement, however, we invite the person to try our program for eight weeks. "No matter how good the program may sound to you," we say, "and no matter how much you might believe it's a good fit, you won't know until you get into it." By taking our full load of classes and one-on-one coaching for two months, new participants learn what we expect and what we will provide. (We also learn about them, of course.) They begin to identify and pursue their goals. After eight weeks, if they've completed the course work in good standing, we ask them to sign the participant agreement. The agreement lists both their and our specific responsibilities. It also establishes a dollar value for what we are providing. We tell them:

If you sign it, we will sign it too. It's a mutual agreement. It obligates us to each other. RISE! will provide the kind of financial, educational, and support services you need to obtain a living-wage job. There's no time limit on our commitment as long as you come to class and continue to do the work. We will work with you for as long as that takes. But you also have an obligation, which we take very seriously. If you sign the agreement, you commit to completing the work, however long it takes, to obtain such a job. If you do not complete your part of the agreement, we have the right to charge you for some of our costs of training and investing in you.

We include these financial consequences for a good reason: if we gave away no-strings-attached training, participants could (and would) walk away at any time with no consequences. This is a pattern that people living in generational poverty repeat over and over again, and it fosters the same kind of self-defeating behaviors that have kept them in poverty. So we quantify the value participants receive by asking them for about 25 percent of what has been spent on them if they drop out.

Some people refuse to sign the agreement and leave the program. In most cases, it's a good decision because they probably didn't expect to finish in the first place. Other people sign but have no intention of finishing, and they drop out after a while. In those cases, we send them a bill with a letter stating how much they owe us.

Quantifying the value has an additional occasional benefit. Once in a while, someone will drop out before graduating but nevertheless land a very good job—and then repay us part of our investment in them.

It's not about the money, of course. It's about holding people accountable for the consequences of their actions. A few folks in the nonprofit and philanthropic worlds have called this accountability draconian. "You can't charge poor people," they've said. "You're pushing them further into debt." We tell such critics that we have never collected from anybody who couldn't afford to pay us—and we know that the cost of pursuing repayment from dropouts almost always exceeds the amount we are likely to recover. We also remind them that our program requires accountability from all stakeholders, not just participants.

The world we live in requires all of us to be accountable. When a nonprofit practices mutual accountability with its participants in a clear and concrete way, there is a better chance they will incorporate it in their belief system and their behaviors.

RISE!'s Accountability with Customer-Employers and the Government

At RISE! we also practice mutual accountability with our customer-employers, and we've found that they embrace the principle. Here's how it works. Our customers hold us accountable for providing qualified employees and reducing their turnover rate, a significant cost savings for them. We hold participants accountable for successfully completing their training and keeping their jobs for at least one year. We hold our customers accountable for hiring our participants who meet their qualifications despite many having spotty résumés and problematic backgrounds. We also expect customers to provide appropriate supervision on the job and to let us know when problems arise so we can help resolve an issue before it threatens retention. In better economic times, when demand for labor exceeded the supply, we were able to charge customer-employers a fee for the benefits of reducing their turnover rate and increasing their workforce diversity. We expect it will be possible to restore that form of financial accountability again once the unemployment rate goes down.

SuperValu, a grocery retailer and distributor headquartered in Minnesota and one of RISE!'s customers, told us they appreciate our approach to accountability because it means they can be confident that they are hiring qualified employees. Ron Tortelli, former senior vice president, explains, "Twin Cities RISE! said if their graduates did not produce, they should not be retained. Additionally, RISE! would try to replace the person who failed; we knew it was a source for more people in the future. So if someone came in and left, we always had a place where we could go and get qualified people from a diverse background. That impressed people within our organization. We had a few failures, but it didn't stop us from going back to RISE! and asking for additional people. To me, RISE!'s commitment to accountability was, and is, really important." So customers recognize the benefit of our commitment to accountability, and their respect for that commitment brings us repeat business.

Government too has been amenable to mutual accountability in the form of a pay-for-performance contract. Each time a participant is placed and retained in a job, we create value through increased tax revenue, decreased subsidies, and reduced corrections (criminal justice) expenses. The government pays us based on the value we create for each successful participant.

Every organization needs the foundation of strong relationships with its stakeholders. Such relationships endure during difficult times, adapt when the situation warrants it, and enable the organization to take advantage of opportunities that arise. Stakeholder relationships that are based on specific, articulated mutual accountability are strong and enduring in this way. Both parties know what they can depend on the other for, and, even more important, both parties know that they can trust the other to meet their obligations. Whether your enterprise is for-profit or nonprofit, if it is based on trust and reliability, you are likely to endure and perhaps even flourish.

HOW HABITAT FOR HUMANITY CREATES MUTUAL ACCOUNTABILITY WITH PARTNERSHIP AND SWEAT EQUITY

The notion of accountability has been a key part of Habitat for Humanity's approach since its founding in Americus, Georgia, in 1976. The principle continues to be fundamental to its mission of financing and building homes with volunteer labor—even today, when Habitat is a worldwide organization headed by Habitat for Humanity International with approximately fifteen hundred U.S. affiliates and five hundred international affiliated programs.

Many people outside Habitat for Humanity have heard of their policy of sweat equity. This version of participant accountability requires home-owners-to-be to work side-by-side with volunteers helping to build their own home or that of another family—before taking possession of their own. In addition, Habitat's principle of accountability guides the relationship between the central organization and local affiliates, as well as relationships between all branches of Habitat and their donors.

Jonathan Reckford, CEO of Habitat for Humanity International, says,

> Deeply embedded in Habitat is this idea of a "hand up but not a hand out." What Habitat is about is trying to treat all of our partner [home owner] families as true partners and that, we believe, gives dignity to the families. It gives them ownership of the success.
>
> It's also important to the volunteers. Volunteers are in relationship with the families. Not doing something *for* somebody but doing something *with* somebody. All across the world (except on very rare occasions) the families do have to put in sweat equity, in terms of actual participation in the building of their homes or their neighbors' homes. We don't want to create dependence, we want to create independence.[1]

Partner families are required to put in a minimum of 200 hours of sweat equity before they can take possession of their own home. The specific number of hours required is set by each local Habitat affiliate: one Massachusetts affiliate, for example, requires 250 hours for a one-adult family and 500 hours for a two-or-more adult family. That may not sound like much of a commitment, but if you're a single parent with a couple of kids and a full-time job and your house is due for completion in seven months, you're committing to working eight extra hours a week before you move in and then paying a mortgage afterward. That's a serious commitment.

Habitat has a basic business model in the United States, though there are variations, primarily overseas.[2] It builds homes using donated labor, money, and materials. Low-income people apply to their local Habitat affiliate to buy the homes, and once they have been selected, they participate in building them. A home is sold with a no-profit mortgage that Habitat holds. The mortgage payments that Habitat receives are then used to build and finance new homes. And the cycle continues.

Habitat homes are built through the mutual accountability of several groups:

- The local Habitat affiliate has the responsibilities of a home construction company, as well as those of a financial institution that issues mortgages, plus it manages a workforce that combines professionals and volunteers. Habitat acquires the home site, raises money for materials and services that volunteers can't provide, chooses and qualifies potential home owners, finances the construction, obtains and organizes volunteers who have varying skill levels, organizes the construction, ensures that the homes meet Habitat's and the community's standards, and issues and manages the mortgages.

- Volunteers and home owners are accountable for most of the construction labor.

- Donors assume accountability for providing cash and, often, materials.

Without the accountability of all these groups, there would be no Habitat houses. This system of mutual accountability not only builds houses, though; it also benefits everyone involved. Home-owners-to-be learn a lot about how a house is built, knowledge that comes in handy when they have a house to maintain. (They also receive specific training in home maintenance separately.) They develop contacts and connections throughout the community—not just social but professional as well. One Massachusetts home owner who was looking to change jobs was offered a position as office manager with the company that poured the foundation for her house.[3]

A certain percentage of the sweat equity can be taken care of by family and friends. This gets the home owner's closest support system invested in this transition to a new life and also brings new volunteers into Habitat.

A Massachusetts home-owner-to-be whose livelihood comes from his plastering and painting business told Habitat that he particularly enjoyed working with the unskilled volunteers. He appreciated their goodwill in coming out to help, of course, but more than that, he learned a lot watching how the construction supervisor taught and encouraged. Now he tries to apply what he learned when he coaches his own crews.

Possibly the biggest benefit of sweat equity to the partner families is the inspiration they receive from seeing perfect strangers showing up to build their house.

Community volunteers benefit from accountability because they become more of a community. "One of the biggest barriers in our society are the socioeconomic barriers. Bringing volunteers together with the homeowner changes everybody involved in the process," says Reckford. Community volunteers come from all walks of life: corporate workers of all levels, stay-at-home parents, members of houses of worship, teachers, construction workers, youth groups, retired people. The list is endless. Barriers of every kind are reduced when people work together for a common goal and take pride in their joint achievement.

Finally, donors find the accountability of sweat equity reassuring. For them, sweat equity means that the recipients of their generosity are hard-working citizens who will value their home and take care of it. Donors often cite sweat equity as a reason for their donation.

Habitat practices accountability in many additional ways inside and outside the organization. They think of it in terms of being in partnership with all of their stakeholders. "Partnership, broadly defined, is critical to everything we do. It's core in our language," says Reckford. "A good partnership always involves mutual accountability."

Every year Habitat for Humanity International and its affiliates officially renew their agreement with one another by signing a covenant, a document that spells out what each can expect from the other and what standards each is expected to meet.

Habitat sees itself as accountable to the community and funders, so it wants to know more precisely what the outcomes of Habitat housing are for neighborhoods, towns, and cities. To this end, Habitat is expanding the metrics it uses. Traditionally it has measured the number of families housed, the numbers of volunteers, mortgages held, and mortgages that have been foreclosed or refinanced. Recently it has begun looking at other long-term effects of its work in terms of property values, crime rates, and other social measures.

This emphasis on mutual accountability has a long history within Habitat. The original mission statement for the Fund for Humanity (the pool of money created by donations and mortgage payments) states: "What the poor need is not charity but capital, not caseworkers but co-workers. And what the rich need is a wise, honorable and just way of divesting themselves of their overabundance."[4]

Clearly Habitat believes that accountability provides benefits that should be shared with all concerned.

ACCOUNTABILITY IS POSSIBLE
ONLY WITH EMPOWERMENT

None of this is to say that creating accountability is easy. When RISE! was launched in 1994, our staff was firmly committed to the principle of mutual accountability, but we encountered a surprising number of challenges putting it into practice. Too many of our participants failed. Too many didn't follow through when they needed to. Too many dropped out even after they'd graduated and gotten a good job.

We were clearly missing something. Our own sense of accountability led us to take a hard look at what was not working. We delved first into our own assumptions. At the time, many people, myself included, assumed that everybody knows what accountability is—what it means and how to be accountable. I thought that people willfully choose to be accountable or not. But as I listened to participants' stories and felt the weight of their experiences with life, it finally hit me: many of our participants didn't have any idea what accountability meant. They'd never practiced it; they had never lived around anyone who practiced it. And furthermore, way down deep in their core, they believed that life wasn't going to get any better tomorrow—no matter what they did. So why behave accountably today?

We realized that to sustain accountability, participants need a positive system of beliefs, feelings, and skills. They need what we call empowerment. Accountability and empowerment are, in fact, complementary principles, two sides of the same coin. We set out to develop Principle #5, Support Personal Empowerment, because as an accountable organization, our job is to do whatever is necessary to help our participants become accountable.

Mutual accountability is the most fundamental of the principles. It should pervade an organization's culture. It should be made clear and explicit through policy and formal agreements. Mutual accountability brings with it many benefits, including a more effective organization and greater value in the minds of stakeholders. Mutual accountability is the foundation for success—for every person and every organization.

QUESTIONS TO HELP YOUR ORGANIZATION APPLY THE PRACTICE OF ACCOUNTABILITY

- Do your participants understand their accountability to your program, or do they think of it as an entitlement? How do you think they would describe its value?

- Do your employees understand and perform accountably with your clients and other stakeholders? Are all responsibilities explicitly defined?

- Is there mutual accountability in each of your stakeholder relationships? Is it one-sided anywhere? Does each stakeholder recognize his or her accountability? Can he or she clearly articulate it?

- How do you communicate accountability? If you do not use a written agreement, would one be helpful? What's the best way to present the agreement so that it motivates, rather than discourages, accountability?

- Does your organization assign a value to the services it provides? Value here means not the cost but the benefit to its recipients. Do the people who need to understand that value really understand it?

- Consider frustration in your organization. Where and when does it occur? Is it consistently associated with certain people or groups? Is there a lack of accountability? Or could there be accountability for the wrong things?

- If there are people who consistently behave in a way that is not accountable, what are the barriers for them? Are there changes in training, coaching, or organizational systems that would help remove those barriers?

5

Principle #5

Support Personal Empowerment

At RISE! we learned the need for empowerment training the hard way. In the first few years, when RISE! was in the pilot stage, we faced a bewildering situation: too many people were dropping out during the program and even after working for a while in the jobs we'd found for them. Something would happen—we often didn't know what—and they were gone. We were enormously frustrated.

We knew we were doing good work. After all, we'd taught our participants the behaviors they needed to succeed in the world of work: Show up on time. Dress appropriately. Look people in the eye. Don't get into arguments. We knew they practiced these things for a while, but then they would revert

Note: Cy Yusten, director of the Empowerment Institute of RISE!, provided much of the content of this chapter, including the example of an empowered and unempowered response to the work situation in Table 5.1.

back to their old behavior. We didn't know why this happened, so we talked to participants and to experts in the field of psychology.

We came to realize that participants couldn't sustain the behaviors of accountability because fundamentally they believed, as one put it, "You're going to get screwed, no matter what you do." So if that's the case—if you think your future is hopeless and you're powerless to do anything about it—why behave like a responsible working person? Another participant described his old self's attitude in this way: "Working for a dollar . . . when I saw people doing it, it's like, those people are nuts." Empowerment is the most personal of the principles. It's imperative to understand what empowerment looks like from the participants' point of view, so I've used their language and their descriptions throughout this chapter.

At RISE! we came to realize that, like other job training programs, we were dealing with participants solely on the behavioral level. But their old belief system, which had helped them survive in the world of concentrated poverty, was there, ready and waiting when a situation became touchy, to undermine everything they'd learned. They didn't know how to change that belief system or their responses to it. So when some incident, large or small, triggered those old beliefs, they didn't have the skills to resist their old patterns of behavior.

We began to assemble a curriculum to teach what we call empowerment—a particular set of cognitive and emotional skills coupled with a positive belief system that enable people to manage their emotions, thinking, and behavior to achieve positive, long-term life goals. Our empowerment training is based on research in two areas of psychology: emotional intelligence and cognitive behavioral therapy. Popularized in the 1990s by Daniel Goleman, emotional intelligence is the ability to identify, assess, and manage the emotions of oneself, of others, and of groups.[1] A large body of research has shown that training in emotional intelligence improves people's health and interactions with others. In organizations, emotional intelligence training increases productivity and morale.[2] Cognitive behavioral therapy (CBT) is a talking therapy that, among other things, teaches a goal-oriented system of techniques to help patients address problems of dysfunctional emotions, behaviors, and cognitions. It has been shown to be effective with a variety of problems, including mood, anxiety, personality, eating, substance abuse, and psychotic disorders.[3]

We developed our initial empowerment curriculum with the help of Steven Stosny, a forerunner in the application of emotional intelligence and CBT to situations outside therapy, such as work and education. Over the years, we have refined the RISE! program based on new research in emotional intelligence, cognitive restructuring, brain function, and working with people who have backgrounds of generational poverty.

If all of this seems a bit elaborate for what some think of as a jobs training program, consider this: a successful RISE! participant went from thinking that way when he joined the program to saying at graduation, "You gotta develop the person before you can develop a potential employee." Our experience has shown that he's absolutely right.

RISE! participants work with empowerment training throughout their time at RISE! They take empowerment classes and get individual coaching from a professional coach. They practice their empowerment skills within the culture of our organization, whether they are in a computer skills or speechcraft class. They continue to get coaching in empowerment when they are on the job. We now have fewer dropouts because the practice of empowerment sustains our people through the tough times.

Our approach of specifically teaching empowerment as a skill is rare in the world of nonprofits, although it's much needed. Empowerment is challenging to teach, but for many participants, the success of everything they do depends on it.

For change to endure, many people must transform themselves. They must stop feeling hopeless about their future and start seeing better possibilities within their grasp, to stop feeling powerless and start taking responsibility for their actions.

Many organizations talk about empowerment as a feeling of self-worth, competence, and optimism about the future. They believe that the feeling is a powerful by-product that develops as participants progress through programs, learning skills and meeting goals. With some groups of clients, that may work just fine. In the case of Habitat, for example, it takes significant inner and outer resources to succeed in the application process and be chosen as a partner family. Because of the rigorous selection process, home-owners-to-be already have at least some sense of their own ability to create a positive future, so the seeds of empowerment fall on fertile soil.

But for participants at many other organizations, the organization must be much more deliberate and systematic about teaching the skills that enable participants to become high-functioning people who achieve their goals. Many participants have to overcome beliefs and feelings that have kept generation after generation stuck in poverty, and nonprofits can't help them to do this just by teaching other skills and expecting empowerment to follow. We also have to teach empowerment specifically. Only then are our participants open to beliefs and behaviors that serve their long-term self-interest.

HOW GENERATIONAL POVERTY DAMAGES PERSONAL EMPOWERMENT

Like RISE!'s participants, many of the people who are served by other nonprofits are the product of two or more generations of poverty. Nonprofit leaders need to understand the differences between generational and situational poverty. That knowledge is critical to all program development, but it is particularly important in developing empowerment training that enables participants to achieve their life goals.

As I touched on in Chapter One, people raised in a culture of generational poverty have had experiences throughout their life that reinforce a belief that their future will be no better than the present. In poor, dangerous neighborhoods, deferred gratification doesn't make sense. Tomorrow you might get shot or beaten up. Why save money? Why go to school? But you can't get out of poverty if you let your emotions dictate your actions or if you are unable to delay gratification. You have to believe that you can overcome your problems through your own actions and decisions.

In cultures of generational poverty, children receive negative messages: "You're no good" or "You'll never do better than your no-account brother," for example. Some of RISE!'s participants report hearing these sorts of comments often as children. One recalls, "My stepdad came into my life when I was four years old. From day one, he told me I was stupid, I was crazy. I'd never have anything, never be anything. . . . I remember feeling so hurt, being so young and feeling so hurt." Hurts like these—we call them core hurts—can be absorbed into a person's belief system, where they affect behavior long after the original incident has passed.

People suffering under situational poverty due to a particular event like losing a job or immigrating are more likely to have grown up with the experience of seeing their actions make a positive difference. According to Ruby Payne, author of *A Framework for Understanding Poverty*, they are also more likely to have family and friends who encourage their development. They are more open to trying suggestions that their coaches or teachers make. They have the language to express their problems and can process what has happened to them. They may still struggle, but they have choices, skills, self-awareness, and hope.[4]

The issue of language and communication is critical. One RISE! participant pointed to this problem when he explained, "I was raised in an environment that the average male, their vocabulary consisted of, 'What's up? Just chillin'. . . . We only knew how to communicate through anger and violence." And when you don't use words to communicate, you don't learn how to do so. According to Payne, those who come from generational poverty typically have a vocabulary far below the average adult's vocabulary. One of the most important tasks of empowerment training is to teach participants how to describe their beliefs, thoughts, and feelings so that they can become aware of them and choose the ones that serve them best.

For many people who have grown up in generational poverty, the essential ideas of empowerment—that a better future is possible for you and that you have the power to influence that future for the better—are so foreign that they're hard to grasp. Their experiences and the messages they received as children have taught them otherwise. Their culture has not even provided them with the language to discuss these concepts. To break the cycle of generational poverty, nonprofits must teach participants the language and skills they need to transform their belief system to one that will serve their long-term self-interest.

TRADITIONAL SOFT-SKILLS VERSUS EMPOWERMENT TRAINING

Employers want workers who "have a good attitude" and "can work with the team." For that reason, many antipoverty programs teach what are known as soft skills in addition to traditional hard skills. Hard skills are the specific technical skills required for the job, such as basic computer skills or machine operations. Soft skills, also called people skills, are the social skills that help people function in a workplace—techniques for better communication and appropriate etiquette, for example.

The trouble with traditional soft skills training is that it doesn't last. This is because it targets only behavior:

- Instead of being late for work, be prompt.

- Instead of coming to work with a chip on your shoulder, avoid heated arguments.

- Instead of looking like a slob, dress for success in clothes that are appropriate for the job and the company's culture.

These are all good behaviors. They make sense, and they're fairly easy to communicate. Participants understand them, and if they're highly motivated, they'll work very hard to behave in the approved manner. But then something happens that triggers a person's old feelings and lack of emotional self-control, and he or she reverts to an old behavior. Often the result is that this person quits or gets fired.

This happens because the new behavior is incongruent with this person's fundamental beliefs. He believes, for example, that if his supervisor looked at him in an odd way, it was because that supervisor is a jerk, or because the company is racist, or because all bosses are unfair. And anyway, he thinks, it doesn't matter if he gets to work on time, because people don't like him and they never will.

This belief system may have functioned as a survival mechanism for some people as they grew up, but it is an enormous obstacle to rising out of poverty. And while soft skills training can help people put those beliefs aside and integrate into a workplace in the short term, it doesn't have long-term staying power because this training doesn't change that original belief system.

When people learn to be empowered, however, they do change their belief system. And they come to understand the connection between their belief system, their thoughts, their feelings, their behaviors—and the consequences that will affect their life, for better or worse. Figure 5.1 illustrates the rela-

Figure 5.1 Empowerment Framework

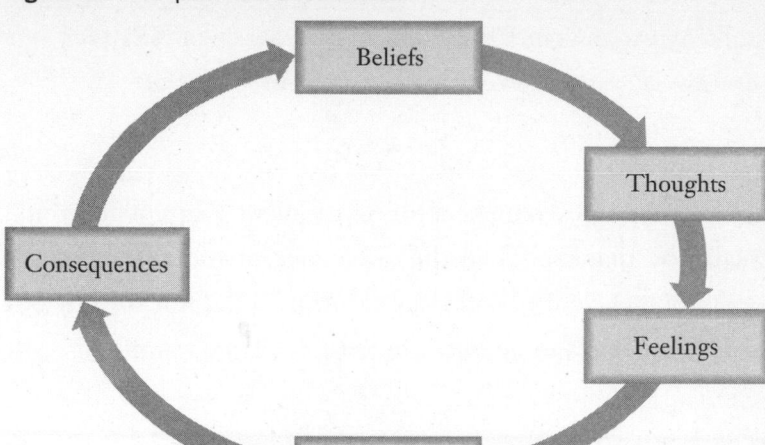

tionships in this system. Our beliefs about life influence our thoughts about a particular situation. The way we think about a situation generates certain feelings. Those feelings in turn influence how we behave, and our behavior changes the ultimate outcome of the situation—the consequences. Those consequences influence our belief system. And the cycle begins again.

The most important part of empowerment—that which creates the most power—is the realization that our beliefs, thoughts, feelings, and behaviors are all within our control. Understanding this gives people a sense of internal power, which leads to an improved sense of self-worth and self-confidence. These, in turn, sustain people as they practice behaviors that enable them to maintain relationships, hold jobs, and function at peak capability.

Here's another way to look at the dynamics of empowerment. Most people would agree that an event (E) plus our reaction (R) to that event leads to an outcome (O):[5]

$$E + R = O$$

RISE! empowerment training modifies that equation in a small way that makes all the difference in the world. In our equation, an event (E) plus our reaction (R), influenced by our beliefs (B), leads to an outcome (O):

$$E + R^{(B)} = O$$

That B (that is, our beliefs) is the most powerful part of the equation because it's the leverage point for changing the whole system. We may have no control over the initial event, but we can change our beliefs about that event. With new beliefs, we can perceive different possible outcomes. When we believe that our reaction can change the outcome—when we believe, in fact, that through our reactions, we have the power to change the outcome—we have motivation to learn new skills for reacting. When we change our reaction, we influence the outcome. We have become more hopeful, more accountable, and more willing to take on new challenges and opportunities. We gain the power to build a future.

All of this builds a new, positive belief system, which is the strongest weapon against the hopelessness of generational poverty. At the heart of this belief system is the core value of empowerment—the precept that everyone is lovable, valuable, and important. The belief system of empowerment is based on three key precepts:

- You are lovable, valuable, and important.

- You can change your behavior.

- Your behavior can change for the better how your life goes.

The Vocabulary of Empowerment

People who grow up in a culture of generational poverty tend to have much smaller vocabularies than the rest of the adult population. Empowerment training gives people essential language to describe values, situations, beliefs, feelings, and actions. Here are key terms:

Core value—the essential precept of empowerment, the birthright that everyone is lovable, valuable, and important

Core hurt—painful experiences that can gradually erode that feeling of core value

Power mode/weak mode—behavior that arises when either core value or core hurt experiences are consciously or sub-consciously activated

Source: Definitions from S. Stosny, *The Powerful Self: A Workbook of Therapeutic Self-Empowerment* (North Charleston, S.C.: Book Surge, 2003).

Empowerment also teaches specific self-awareness and self-regulation skills that enable participants to:

- Perceive more options for their behavior
- Choose the option most likely to optimize their long-term self-interest
- Implement that choice

While these outcomes may sound simple, straightforward, and, possibly, coldly intellectual, the process of achieving them is rigorous and deeply emotional. You have to deal with your core hurts, the painful experiences that erode your new belief system and therefore your behavior. Every coach teaches, challenges, and supports this transformation as needed. But even so, participants need persistence, introspection, and courage. One participant described how she got herself to confront these issues: "The stuff the coach makes you face . . . I mean, he didn't badger it out of you. But you really couldn't say, 'I don't want to talk about that.' Because how are you going to deal with it if you don't talk about it?"

So how does all this theory play out in real life? Table 5.1 presents two ways to respond to a situation one of our participants could easily face—a boss making a remark that sounds insulting. In real life, of course, this incident would take about a minute. But a lot can go on in a minute.

Results? In the first scenario, no amount of soft skills training could have prevented these reactions because they stem from core hurts. The working relationship deteriorates, and the employee gets known as someone who has a bad attitude.

Table 5.1 Responding to an Employment Situation Without and With Empowerment

EVENT	RESPONSE	
	My Thoughts and Feelings	**My Response (Behaviors)**
WITHOUT EMPOWERMENT		
I had yesterday off because I had so much overtime logged in, but like always, I came into work this morning right on time.	Thoughts: I like my working style. I always give 100 percent and sometimes more. Feelings: Personal pride	
When I walked in the door, I saw my boss throwing equipment into the truck.	Feelings: My gut clenched immediately. I started getting nervous and tense. Thoughts: Oh no! I've seen him throw stuff before. This isn't going to be good.	
He looked up at me and said, "Hey, Sleeping Beauty, . . ."	Feelings: More nervousness Thoughts: Is he joking with me or serious? I don't like the way this feels.	I watched his face closely to see if he was kidding or serious. No smile. He's upset.
". . . I'm glad you could make it."	Thoughts: He's being sarcastic. So he's not only upset, he's going to take it out on me. Feelings: Anxious, frustrated, unappreciated	I don't say anything bad, although I have a couple of things I'd like to say.
I said, "What? It's only eight o'clock. Is there a problem?"	Thoughts: I better defend myself. I'm on time. What's up with him? Feelings: Higher anxiety, frustration	Since he was giving me attitude, I gave him some back by adding an edge to my voice and gestures to show how wrong this was.

(Continued)

Table 5.1 (*Continued*)

EVENT	RESPONSE	
	My Thoughts and Feelings	**My Response (Behaviors)**
"Yeah, there is," he said. "We have a huge job that has to be done today. We've got to be loaded and out of here in ten minutes. Grab your gear and let's go."	Thoughts: So it's all my fault. And to think I could have just taken more time off. I've got all that overtime built up anyway. That would have served him right. If he's going to treat me like this, I'll just show him. Feelings: Unappreciated, defensive, hostile	I start putting equipment in the truck, but I take my own sweet time about it. I even take a little extra time by claiming to need to stop in the bathroom before we leave.

WITH EMPOWERMENT

I had yesterday off because I had so much overtime logged in, but like always, I came into work this morning right on time.	Thoughts: I like my working style. I always give 100 percent and sometimes more. Feelings: Personal pride	
When I walked in the door, I saw my boss throwing equipment into the truck.	Thoughts: I've seen this behavior before. The boss is stressed today. I know it's not about me, but I wonder what is going on? Feelings: Some nervousness	
He looked up at me and said, "Hey, Sleeping Beauty . . ."	Feelings: Still a little nervous Thoughts: I know he's just giving me a hard time, but I also know he doesn't mean anything by it. But he's already having a bad day.	I watched his face closely, and I can see the tension he's feeling.

Table 5.1 *(Continued)*

EVENT	RESPONSE	
	My Thoughts and Feelings	**My Response (Behaviors)**
". . . I'm glad you could make it."	Thoughts: He's under so much pressure he probably needs help. I'll bet he is really glad to see someone here that he can count on. Feelings: Curious about what the problem is and still a little anxious	I don't say anything. I just try to listen and learn about what the real problem is.
I said, "What? It's only eight o'clock. Is there a problem?"	Thoughts: Maybe I can lighten up the moment by reminding him that we can still get an early start on whatever the issue is. Feelings: Compassion about his feelings, confidence that we can solve this problem	I softened the tone of my voice so he would know I was ready and able to help.
"Yeah, there is, he said. "We have a huge job that has to be done today. We've got to be loaded and out of here in ten minutes. Grab your gear and let's go."	Thoughts: Wow! So that's what it's all about. I'll bet we can be loaded in five minutes because I know where everything is that we'll need. I'm glad that I can help with this. Feelings: Confident, capable, assured of my personal value	I give him a smile and a thumbs-up and quickly grab the stuff that we will need. I work quickly and confidently. I can already see some of his tension draining away. We're headed out the door within minutes and on the way to solve another problem.

If it happens often enough, the employee loses a job and the employer loses an employee who actually was doing good work and incurs the cost of replacing him.

In the second scenario, the employee doesn't feel attacked personally. He recognizes that the supervisor's feeling aren't based on his behavior. He controls his emotion so he can deal with the problem productively. And the working relationship strengthens, which benefits both employer and employee.

Some people might say that the employee in the second scenario has a good attitude. But at RISE! we've learned that "attitude" actually encompasses a cycle of beliefs, thoughts, feelings, and behaviors that can support or sabotage a person's success. We've learned that empowerment training can teach people skills that enable them to change those beliefs, thoughts, feelings, and behaviors. Using those empowerment skills, they can change their reactions to external events over which they have no control and influence outcomes for the better. Their belief system no longer undermines the important soft skills they've learned about working with people. Instead, they are empowered to take those soft skills into the workplace and create a better life for themselves.

TEACHING EMPOWERMENT AT RISE!

At RISE! teaching empowerment isn't just about the curriculum. It is also about understanding the unique needs of our participants, the challenges they face, and creating a culture that is aware of those needs and provides appropriate support.

Generational poverty is only one obstacle that people must overcome in order to develop empowerment. Events have a way of throwing empowerment learning off course. Things will be going pretty well for a participant, when he's suddenly told to leave the apartment where he's been sleeping on the couch. Or he's arrested—possibly for no real reason or for something he didn't do. Empowerment can help a lot when life gets tough. But difficult situations can undermine new beliefs and skills and reinforce an old belief system.

In addition, people who are transforming their lives through empowerment often lose their old social support. A participant who rejects negative behaviors that are commonplace for his or her old group is told, "You're a fool. Get out of here." And a participant who finally refuses to tolerate verbal abuse from his or her partner or family may get assaulted. A person can feel very alone.

Our task at RISE! is to support participants through these events and transitions while holding them accountable for continuing to practice the skills of empowerment. Each participant's coach is responsible for maintaining that critical balance. Participants also get support from peers, staff, and outside support when it is needed.

Coach support can seem pretty tough when you're on the receiving end, as one RISE! graduate recalls:

> I was getting burnt out. Burnt out with the effort. Burnt out with trying to do something new. And my coach said, "You don't have to worry about computers. You don't have to worry about typing, because you're suspended. And in that suspension, you have to take an extra class. You have to take another empowerment class." . . . About two weeks into that class, the light bulb literally went on. I got it! I

finally got it. I'm learning all these new skills. I'm learning different concepts on how to think and how to live and how to believe in myself, and I'm not applying them. That's why I'm going back into weak mode, going back into the stinkin' thinkin' because I'm not applying this new thing that I've learned that's going to help me.

After the light bulb, persistence and determination take over. The same man continues:

I started hunting for jobs more. I started coming to school when there's no school to get on that computer to type. My computer was the one in the corner. I'm in that corner so you don't how many words I'm typing. You don't know whether I'm getting the computer application classes. Because I was always one or two or three steps behind the class. I got in that corner, and I cried many a times, and I'd play it off so people couldn't see the tears.

Frustration with computer skills reduced this man to tears. Still, by choosing a spot in the corner, he found a way to persist and save face. He graduated and went on to a productive life. Being suspended and going through one more empowerment class seems to have made the difference for him.

Our empowerment class curriculum begins with the self—the language and skills of emotional self-awareness. We build on self-awareness with skills of self-regulation and self-motivation. Participants begin to accept their own intrinsic self-worth, and they see the power they have to control and motivate themselves. Then we expand the training outward to encompass others.

We teach the empathy that participants will need for providing good customer service, understanding the emotional currents within groups, and seeing the relationships within an organization. Finally, we teach social skills such as influence, communication, negotiation, and teamwork.

Once or twice a week, empowerment classes are led by an experienced instructor, many of them graduates of our program. It has to be someone who is already empowered, because participants will see right through anyone who is faking. Instructors become a model for an empowered person who has demonstrated the perseverance to transform himself.

One of the ways we help participants learn empowerment and overcome their individual challenges is by making sure that empowerment is part of our organization's culture. Regardless of his or her job, every staff member at RISE! is required to take the initial empowerment course. Many take additional courses as well, and our coaches take them all. Our employees use the language of empowerment in all their interactions. If you go into any class—math, computer applications, or customer service—you might hear someone exclaim, "I can't get this! It's too tough," and a fellow classmate or instructor will remind the person that he is reverting to "weak mode" thinking. Those words are part of the vocabulary of empowerment. They remind participants to use the skills they've learned to get back into "power mode" and think positively about their ability to deal with the problem.

One participant described it this way: "I did not give up. I said, 'I'm gonna get this. I'm gonna make this happen. Yeah. Excuse me. I'm gonna make it happen.' The encouragement here. The people here. Wow!"

Because it is part of our culture, empowerment training is constantly reinforced and continues throughout a participant's time with RISE! Underlying everything we do and teach is the core value that everyone is valuable, lovable, and important. Everyone. That includes yourself, your customers, the people you work with, and the people you work for. Everyone at RISE! tries to model this principle.

At RISE! empowerment is more than a skill that is taught: it is something that every member of our staff must practice. Teaching empowerment in classes is necessary and useful, but it isn't enough on its own. As an organization, we must create a culture that reinforces what is learned in those classes and be sensitive to the challenges our participants face. We must help them cope so that once they learn how to become empowered, they know how to stay that way.

THE TRANSFORMATIVE POWER OF EMPOWERMENT TRAINING

We first came to empowerment as a practical matter: it was the missing piece we needed for participants to succeed in their training and in the workplace. But it is so much more.

Being part of one of the achievement celebrations that we conduct every ten weeks is extraordinarily moving. Hundreds of friends, parents, significant others, and children fill the seats. For many participants, this is the first time in their lives that they have completed something they started. I have seen tough ex-convicts cry as they talk about the way their lives have changed since they came to believe that they are lovable, valuable, and important. Here is what two of our participants have said:

> Empowerment has helped me find hope. It has helped strengthen me. . . . Empowerment has made me a better father because I'm not angry anymore, and I'm not hurt anymore. So I am able to spend real quality time with my children without the interruptions of negative thoughts popping in my head. . . . In just over a year, I went from depression to a place of peace. I went from being homeless to living in a house with my name on the lease. I went from being underemployed to having a full-time job with medical, dental, and a 401k plan. And the greatest thing is I went from being single to being married!

> A year ago, my life was going nowhere, nothing was happening for me. I didn't care about me because I felt no one else did. . . . Feelings of defeat made me think that there was nothing I could do to make my life better and that I had to settle for whatever was thrown my way. . . . In knowing my role and responsibility as a mother, I knew it was time to make a real change in my life. . . . Never again will I be bullied into silence or allow myself to be made a victim. I am no longer accepting anyone's definition of my life. I'm defining myself.

These are just two of the many people who have found empowerment through RISE! When participants finally experience true empowerment, it changes their lives and gives them a new respect for themselves and for others.

THE ROAD TO EMPOWERMENT

Nothing can illustrate the transformative power of empowerment training more clearly than the stories of our participants, told in their own words. With that in mind, two of our graduates tell the stories of their lives before and after going through RISE!'s program:

Mike's Story

I was born and raised on the West Side of Chicago, unfortunately in a drug-infested, poverty-stricken neighborhood. The oldest of five. My father was a drug dealer on the West Side. My mother, of course, was at a regular job, worked and provided. My father was in and out of our lives. There were moments when we [felt] like we had an enemy, literally. [We'd come back from a family reunion] and the TVs are gone and our ten-speed bicycles were gone. Things that we valued as kids. It's all gone due to drug use.

We were having Thanksgiving dinner [in 1989, when I was in my early twenties] when my dad kicked in the door. He was yelling, with the syringe still in his arm. He was shouting, "I'm going to kill everybody! I'm going to kill everybody!"

I knew all along it would come to that. Me and my dad had had several fistfights, and so I'd bought a gun hot off the streets. I ran upstairs to get it. When I came back down, he saw me with the gun and ran out of the house. I caught up with him like a block away from my house and shot him four times. But I didn't kill him.

Imagine, in a drug-infested neighborhood with gangs, you are known as the guy who shot his own dad. I didn't want to do it, but I was kind of put in that position to protect my own family. Every gang wanted me to be with them because of my reputation. Instead, I started selling drugs. Then it was the usual path. You start selling, and then you eventually start being your biggest customer. More violence comes along, and soon life becomes one big hustle.

An incident that occurred after he finished junior high school in 1981 stands out in Mike's memory because of its significant and negative contribution to his core hurts. For high school, Mike and some of his buddies were bused to an excellent suburban school, thanks to arrangements made by the principal of the inner-city school near his home:

> I truly believe that [our] principal's intentions were well, but I don't think he could see the big picture. The quality of education we were getting in our inner-city [school] didn't prepare us to exist in a high school that was in the northwest suburbs. We were in class wondering, "What is this teacher talking about? We never heard of this."
>
> I think that's where the voices of incompetency or you're illiterate or you can't get things done [came from]. That whole experience set a lot of people up. We thought it was us. We didn't understand that we just weren't prepared.
>
> So we ended up coming back to the worst high school in Chicago. It was all downhill from there. You'd experienced that feeling of not being able to keep up with

grades. Then you go live in a community that says you're never going to be anything. And you're in a home that says you're gonna be just like your dad. Now I'm sixteen. I'm thinking of all these voices. I just said, "Well, let the prophecy be. Why try?"

Over the next couple of decades, Mike worked in a steel mill for a while. He made good money there but eventually started using heroin and cocaine like others on his crew did. He spent time in prison. He fathered four children by different girlfriends. He got sober and clean, then was hospitalized for depression, then started doing drugs again. In 2001 he was referred to RISE! by his treatment program:

Certain things that I was missing, that I couldn't understand or figure out, RISE! taught me. At the end of one of our [empowerment] sessions, I was leaving, and my coach said, "You've got potential, man, but you've gotta get your emotions together." I thought, "Hey, you just met me. How do you know?" And then he would just talk to me about the empowerment, and I thought, "Yeah. Valuable." See, these things—I always felt they were there, but I just didn't know how to connect to it.

I've been hearing all my life, "Change, and here's how." But Twin Cities RISE! not only says, "Change, here's how," but they sold me on the, "Here's why you should change." [My coach] sold me on the package of the end result and understanding why that end result is so important: "You will have a healthy relationship with yourself" [he said]. "You will believe in yourself. You will trust yourself."

After graduating from RISE! Mike was hired at a charitable organization, where he was promoted from front desk worker to program specialist to case worker:

> I value the accountability. These people expect to see me or hear from me on a weekly basis. Also, I take value in being recognized as a responsible, dependable father, brother, son, case manager.
>
> I provide support for my children—not just financially, but emotionally and spiritually. They can call on me, whereas before they wouldn't have anything to do with me.

Sharon's Story

> I knew that my dad used to beat my mom. He'd drink too much, and she'd be trying to keep him quiet because he might wake us. That's how they got divorced when I was about twelve. My mom woke us up in the middle of the night, and it was raining. It's like something out of a movie. She was shoving five kids in their pajamas out to the old station wagon in a storm, hopping in the car. My dad woke up. He heard us. Tried to make us get out of the car. We're screaming and everything.
>
> My mom, she was awesome. [She] raised five kids by herself. We grew up in the projects in North Minneapolis. [She worked the night shift as a nurse's aide.] She'd get off from Hennepin County [Medical Center] at 7:20 in the morning, and her second job was in a nursing home. I just used to think, *Man, she's just working herself to death for her*

kids. So when I was about fourteen, I decided then that I was going to help out.

So what I did was I went to Burger King on Broadway in North Minneapolis, and I lied about my age to get my first job. [You had to be fifteen to work until closing time.]

I smoked my first joint when I was fourteen on the railroad tracks at the back of the high school. My girlfriend gave it to me, and I never looked back. I smoked weed morning, noon, and night. When I was fifteen, I got pregnant. And I had plans for my life. I remember the day that me and my girlfriend rode the bus over to the clinic to find out if I was pregnant. And we're on the bus and we're like fifty-fifty, you're not, fifty-fifty, you are. Of course, it came back positive, and I just cried. I just cried. It's pretty ironic that earlier that same day, I'd been trying to get up the nerve to ask Mom for birth control.

My mom was from the old school. "You got yourself pregnant, so you're having that kid," she said. She called a big family meeting right away. I'm only fifteen years old, and I'm scared out of my wits. I'm thinking they're calling a meeting to show me that they support me. She called the meeting to tell my two younger sisters, "This is what you don't want to be. This is how you don't want to end up." I was crushed. And at that very moment, that's when I decided that I was going to not turn out to be how everybody just knew I was going to turn out to be. I'm not going to have all these babies biting at my heels and collect welfare forever. That's not going to happen. I stayed at my high school.

[I got into the work-study program at school.] They got me a part-time job at a big corporation. My kid was a year and a half when I graduated from high school.

After that I just worked and worked all the time because I had Bobby, and I had to take care of him. [I had low-paying, part-time jobs and never made a living wage.] Still, I never once cheated on welfare. Always told when I worked. It was so hard because, of course, the more money you [earn, the more they deduct from your check]. So you never quite make ends meet. But I did what I needed to do.

Fast-forward to full-time jobs. One of my favorites was at [a large, Minneapolis-based corporation] as a secretary for the quality assurance department. I was so happy with this job.

The drinking and the drugging started to get in my way. I remember one time when I went on a bender over the weekend, and, you know, I didn't go to work for three or four days, probably a week. And they were calling me with messages: "Oh, we're worried. We're worried." I just thought, well, I can't just walk back up in there all like hoity-toity. I've gotta say something happened. So I said I got in a car accident and that I was so out of it that I wasn't able to call in. And showed up with crutches and everything. I pray for forgiveness from God for all that.

I thought that someday I was going to retire from there. But then they up and sold themselves to another company and did a lot of restructuring. I [had] worked so hard and so long that when I lost my job, I just went into a downward spiral. Just went spinning out of control.

That lasted over twelve years. I did everything except shoot up, and I didn't do that because I've always been afraid of needles.

I had an escort service. Me and the other girls, we all worked together because we were all doing the same things. We wanted to get high and pay our babysitters to keep our kids for weeks at a time.

If I [had] saved half the money that I made between the escorts, the dating, and I sold drugs, too. . . . Geez. But you don't think about a retirement plan. But I also kept saying to myself that I wasn't going to be doing this forever.

The spiral stopped for me two months before my fortieth birthday [when I was convicted of assault]. Two years before, a guy had tried to rape me, and I had stabbed him. I knew if I had left him, he would have bled to death. So I stayed, and I held pressure on the wound until the ambulance got there. But the police got there first, and they knocked down the door. Then the guy proceeded to jump up like a jack-in-the-box, screaming, "She's killing me, she's killing me." They gave me five years, but I only had to serve eighty days before my probation.

I did forty days in jail, and then I was sent to the workhouse. I think I'm the only person on earth thanking God for sending me to jail. It was his way of telling me, "This is your chance." I turned forty in the women's workhouse. Except for not being allowed to see my daughter, it was the best birthday I ever had. It was the first birthday that I hadn't been high [since I was a kid]. I was happy to be alive and sober and have what was left of my right mind.

When I got out of the workhouse, I knew the path I wanted to take. I had been sober for almost a year when I found Twin Cities RISE! I was working for a temp service and getting food stamps and medical assistance from welfare.

The best part of RISE! was the coach who taught empowerment. He pulled no punches. His empowerment made you look down at the gut of you. Who knew about core hurts and core values? I had never heard those words before. He made me face all the stuff, all the choices I'd made, my family relationships, everything.

I took three Foundations of Empowerment classes, along with all the developmental classes—typing and word processing, mock interviews, office machines, how to use a computer, all that stuff. It all went hand in hand. Once I started to develop as a person and [think more clearly], then I could concentrate on getting my typing speed up, getting my keystroke up on the ten-key, writing a business letter, sending off thank-you cards after an interview. You learn all of that stuff.

Empowerment teaches you that, "Look, this is who you were meant to be. And we're going to give you the tools to be who you are supposed to be." [But] you have to do the work.

After graduating from RISE! Sharon accepted a job at SuperValu, where she has now worked for more than five years. She is taking night classes at a private college, studying for her bachelor's degree in human resource management.

Today RISE! offers more than twenty different classes in a wide range of academic subjects and occupational skills. Yet none is more essential than empowerment. It provides the readiness for learning and lays the foundation for success. It enables individuals to be accountable, to be willing to learn, to change their lives and, ultimately, to escape poverty. It changes lives.

EMPOWERMENT IN ACTION: HOW OTHER ORGANIZATIONS HAVE PUT EMPOWERMENT TO WORK FOR THEM

At RISE! we have experienced enormously positive results by teaching empowerment to our participants. In fact, we believe that empowerment is so crucial to every human being's success that we have extended our curriculum beyond our own program to people in widely different venues—from the working world to prisons to middle schools and universities. We accomplish this through the Empowerment Institute, a separately managed division within RISE! that conducts training sessions and licenses our empowerment curriculum.

Through the Empowerment Institute, we have provided empowerment training to supervisors and employees at work sites to increase their productivity. We offer it at other non-profit organizations and to poor, single mothers who are in college. We train teachers at charter and public schools who deal with especially challenging students, most of whom have the same problems with self-esteem, accountability, and emotional regulation that our participants do. We teach university students to increase their persistence toward graduation, and we teach empowerment in prisons. Early results with prisoners indicate that there are fewer discipline problems among those who have been trained in empowerment.

Each organization uses empowerment training in its particular way to best serve its participants, as you'll see in the three examples that follow.

Jeremiah Program: Requiring Empowerment Training Before Admission

Jeremiah Program, an antipoverty nonprofit, was founded in the late 1990s in Minneapolis. Its goal is to break the cycle of poverty by giving low-income single mothers with young children the support they need to earn a college degree, maintain a living-wage job, and prepare their kids for public school success. The program provides safe, affordable apartments on campuses in several cities, along with life skills classes, counseling, child care, and early childhood education. The program believes so strongly in its participants' need for empowerment that it provides empowerment training to applicants before participants even enter the program, so those applicants can succeed with Jeremiah and ultimately in their lives.

Jeremiah women carry a daunting load: they go to college, work part time, take care of their children, and go to classes in financial management, parenting, career planning, and more. Their commitment requires strength and resilience—all the more so because of the painful experiences that typically bring them to the program.

Gloria Perez, CEO of Jeremiah Program, took RISE!'s empowerment train-the-trainer course in September 2001, with the thought of making it part of the classes that Jeremiah women take while they're in residence. Over the next few years, Jeremiah staff came to realize that if participants learned the language and skills of empowerment before they moved to housing on campus, they'd be better prepared to succeed in the program and in the Jeremiah community. Empowerment is now part of the admission process.

To become part of Jeremiah Program, a woman must first apply and have an initial interview. If she qualifies, she's invited to take an empowerment class once a week for sixteen weeks, at no charge. After completing week 12, she's qualified for her final interview, and if that's successful, she's admitted to the program. "So," says executive director Vickie Williams, "you invest three months of your life, and you don't have a clue whether you're going to be accepted."

Some women walk away once they hear about the requirement. A few drop out after they've started. Perez considers that a good thing: "If they think after taking some empowerment classes that this is mumbo-jumbo or this is not what they want or need, they're probably not a good fit for our program." Many women state in the final interview that whether they're admitted or not, they're glad to have taken the empowerment classes.

Weekly empowerment classes teach the women who apply to Jeremiah Program that a better future is possible for them and their children and that they have the power to achieve that future. The applicants learn methods to manage their emotions, thinking, and behavior so they can achieve positive, long-term life goals.

The most important thing they learn, according to Perez, is their core value: that everyone is lovable, valuable, and important. This leads to some very interesting conversations: "They get that, they believe it. Then when you say to the mom, 'Now, your baby's father, who's in jail or who is abusive to you or whatever, also has core value,' their immediate reaction is, 'No he doesn't; he's a jerk.'" Perez continues, "While you might understand why they feel that way, it creates a great opportunity to talk about the fact that, no, that person who has been hurtful or has made bad choices indeed still has core value, but because he's operating maybe out of his core hurts, he continues to hurt people or hurt himself. So it's been very interesting to be in that dialogue with women and help them find compassion and recognize that the only thing they can control is themselves, their thoughts, their feelings, their actions. That's very liberating."

As part of their empowerment training, Jeremiah women learn how to regulate their own emotional responses, which helps them deal with highly charged relationships—whether it's with their children's father or fathers, their own parents, or other close but difficult relationships. In addition, these skills enable them to live in a community where everyone has core hurts, and the simplest act—like someone moving your laundry basket—can be perceived as hostile and trigger old beliefs and old behaviors.

Empowerment has become a part of the working culture at Jeremiah Program. Perez thinks the empowerment training that staff members receive helps them in their official capacities—giving and receiving feedback, for example, in ways that are more productive. "Those values—that everyone can grow and change and has something to contribute—make it a very positive environment." She believes that empowerment makes Jeremiah Program a good place to work.

Williams has this to say about the value of empowerment training for participants: "When [the women] get two weeks into empowerment, something changes; it's almost miraculous. They start to see that they are not alone and that their situation—meaning poverty—is just a temporary condition."

This gives aspiring Jeremiah women a great jump-start in acquiring the skills they need to thrive as parents, college students, working women, and neighbors in the Jeremiah community.

Junior and Senior High Students: How Empowerment Training Helps with Emotional and Behavioral Problems

Kids who can't take regular classes because of their disruptive behavior aren't just troublemakers. They're often unhappy young people who are struggling with emotional and mental health issues and could be performing better if they had additional social and behavior management skills. They're also expensive for the school system, since students with these disorders require special education resources that their mainstream peers don't.

In 2009, the St. Paul Public Schools began providing empowerment training for all junior and senior high students who are away from their mainstream peers for 60 percent or more of their time in school because of emotional and behavioral issues. They take a weekly thirty-minute empowerment class facilitated by a social worker. Special education teachers participate alongside them, because, says Anne Byer-Rajput, lead empowerment coach for the St. Paul Public Schools, "if the staff aren't acting in an empowered way, forget telling the kids what *they* need to do for power mode or weak mode."

The empowerment tools that resonate most strongly with these students are the concepts of power mode and weak mode. The phrases enter the kids' language quickly and stick. Kids learn that when they're in power mode, they're operating out of the knowledge that they're lovable, valuable, and important. They hear positive messages about themselves inside their heads, have gained self-confidence, and behave in a way that's respectful to themselves but also doesn't interfere with others' needs. They're doing what's in their own long-term best interest, and they're worthy of that. Conversely, when they're in weak mode, they're operating out of their core hurts (memories of deeply hurtful events), they feel like giving up, and they're behaving in ways that hurt themselves or others.

Byer-Rajput recommends that any school system that wants to institute empowerment training should have a position like lead empowerment coach. After all, she says, teachers are learning a new curriculum and implementing it with the toughest kids in the district. Byer-Rajput trains special education teachers who lead the weekly empowerment classes for the students. All the staff who work with these kids attend the weekly classes, so they can incorporate the skills of empowerment into other situations. She provides one-on-one coaching for teachers and cofacilitates the weekly classes as needed. She has also developed a two-year curriculum that breaks the training down into sixty manageable lessons for a population with short attention spans. Ideas come alive as kids watch short clips from movies and videos, delve into newspaper articles, and discover how much of what they are learning in empowerment class is already expressed in the songs they listen to. They learn how to read situations—Is that character in power mode or weak mode?—so they can ask themselves the same question. They probe the meaning of the values they're being taught: Does the convicted murderer who's in hospice care in a prison in New York City have core value? Does he have a right to that care? They find these illustrations compelling enough that those who repeat a class express eagerness to work with these ideas again.

These students also need physical representations of ideas. A favorite exercise for just about everyone who takes an empowerment course is, "Who's in your audience?" We explain it this way. "If your life was a movie or a play, would you want your meanest critics in the front row? Of course not. Well, it's your show. You get to put your supporters in front and move those naysayers who tell you you'll never amount to anything all the way back to the last row. You can even move them out of the theater altogether." Adults do the exercise in their imagination. These students get to act it out, directing their classmates where to stand.

One boy reported, "I went home and used it on Saturday. My uncle's always putting me down, riding me, talking smack about me. My mom said, 'Why you gonna take that from him? Why don't you tell him . . . ,' [and I said] 'I don't need to, Mom. I've already moved him out of my audience.'"

The school system is beginning to collect outcomes data, but it's difficult to isolate the effects of empowerment training because it's not the only intervention at work. Nevertheless, says Byer-Rajput, they're definitely seeing positive results: "The goal is for [the students] to be able to manage themselves in a large, regular class, without a paraprofessional sitting next to them and an intervention room down the hall. . . . [The kids who'd been in the empowerment program for two years] were able to take four mainstream classes a term, . . . which is huge."

The University of Dubuque:
Improving Persistence Rates

The University of Dubuque (UD) is a historically Presbyterian school with approximately sixteen hundred undergraduate and graduate students located in Dubuque, Iowa. Its campus made modest cinema history when it served as a location for a scene in the movie *Field of Dreams.*

Like many other postsecondary institutions, UD struggles to increase persistence rates (the rate at which students continue on to the next semester and then ultimately graduate), particularly for its young men and women from poor, inner-city backgrounds. Its goal is to create culture, language, and support systems that will enable students to succeed in their first year, learning values and behaviors that will carry them through subsequent years at UD and their adult lives. The university is very much in the business of building values and acting in loco parentis. Its leaders see UD as a "diamond university," with the four sides of the diamond being academics, vocation, community, and stewardship. Empowerment is a key part of this initiative.

UD piloted empowerment training with faculty and staff in 2007. Rollout took place in fall 2009, with empowerment training integrated into World View I, a required course. UD judged that a separate empowerment class would feel like too big a burden for students who can feel overwhelmed by homesickness, or the registration process, or the supremely negative inner voice that says, "Why bother? I'm just going to flunk out anyway."

The student mentors who provide support during orientation and tutoring the rest of the year have been trained in empowerment. They use its language and processes to get their protégés through tough times. For example, empowerment teaches that feelings are influenced by thoughts. We can identify our thoughts, challenge them, change them, and ultimately change the feeling. So a mentor might say to a freshman who's feeling overwhelmed and anxious, "Okay, so what's the thought behind that fear? You're worried about flunking out. But you're here today because the admissions department was pretty sure you could make it. And they have a lot of experience."

Students in World View I are encouraged to explore their role in the university community and in the rest of the world. They look at writings by historic figures through the lens of empowerment. Like St. Paul Public School kids, they acquire stories, but their stories come from literature.

UD's faculty receive training in empowerment as well, so that the language of empowerment is spoken and understood across the campus. In the past, says Mark Smith, director of service and leadership, "as students navigated the college experience, they would talk to their advisor or a faculty member, and they'd get the same message—about locus of control, being proactive, making the best of the situation you're in—but it was in a different language [depending on who they were talking to] so it seemed like a different message." Now students hear a message in class that's reinforced by faculty and staff. This is a more powerful way, UD feels, to prepare students to be successful in college and in their later lives.

It's early to have statistically significant data on the results of empowerment training, especially because it's part of a larger initiative. But, says John Stewart, the professor who oversees UD's Diamond Initiative, "UD has been told by varied and well-informed outsiders that we are one of the few schools that really 'gets' how different [the needs of] twenty-first-century higher education [students are]. . . . National data and our experience demonstrate that a high percentage of incoming students now need holistic, intentional intrusive programming in order to persist and graduate. Empowerment is a key part of the programming that we're providing."[6]

Teaching empowerment as a class alone is not nearly as powerful as incorporating it into the institution's culture. That means staff members need to be trained so they buy into it and model its precepts. The vocabulary needs to become part of the language of the institution. Additional coaching or mentoring beyond classes helps individuals embed it into their own issues. Short-term empowerment training alone is good and can certainly have long-term effects. But embracing empowerment as part of the organization's culture is better; it's a more powerful way to achieve long-lasting benefits for both participants and the organization itself.

THE POWER OF EMPOWERMENT TRAINING TO BUILD MORE EFFECTIVE ORGANIZATIONS

Whether in academic education or workplace training and development, organizations too often focus intensely on academic and technical skills, with at most a nod to soft skills training. Traditional soft skills training focuses on teaching new behaviors, but those behaviors tend not to endure because they are incompatible with the person's belief system. Belief systems can and will change as people practice the awareness and self-regulation skills of empowerment—and recognize that they can influence outcomes in their life by changing their response to events over which they have no control.

Unfortunately, our organizations rarely make the financial and emotional investment in building up individuals by addressing deeply held negative beliefs. If we did, we could improve our outcomes significantly—in inner-city schools, universities, and social programs that work with people who come from generational poverty or deal with emotional and behavioral issues. It's an opportunity waiting for our action.

QUESTIONS TO HELP YOUR ORGANIZATION SUPPORT PERSONAL EMPOWERMENT

- Do you know the extent to which negative beliefs affect your participants' ability to succeed? What are you doing to shift those beliefs to positive ones? Are these efforts working?

- Do you rely on a behavior-centered model (traditional soft skills), or do you focus on changing the beliefs of your participants? What can you do to transform your participants' beliefs?

- Does your organizational culture reflect an empowered one? If not, what can you do to transform it? Would empowerment training benefit your participants and staff if you do not already provide it?

6

Principle #6

Create Economic Value from Social Benefit

T hose of us who create social good are all too familiar with the costs of providing our services. Too many of us, however, are unfamiliar with the financial value we create with those same services. That needs to change.

A society that supports organizations that create social benefit is not just doing what is right; it is doing what is smart. That's because every improvement in social good has economic value that benefits participants, state or federal government, or any of a host of other stakeholders. In most cases, we can identify not only who is receiving monetary value, but also by how much—in other words, the specific dollar value of that social benefit. That analysis can provide nonprofit leaders with a powerful tool for managing their organizations and financing social initiatives.

Common Ground is an example of a savvy nonprofit that used the concept of economic value—and specific comparison data—to convince government to change its policy and steer more funding toward the nonprofit's way of addressing homelessness.

It demonstrated that supportive housing is a good financial deal for the government. The apartments it rents to low-income and formerly homeless tenants cost approximately $36 per night to operate. This compares to public expenditures of $54 for a city shelter bed, $74 for a state prison cell, $164 for a city jail cell, $467 for a psychiatric bed, and $1,185 for a hospital bed. The differential between the cost of supportive housing and the cost of alternative methods for housing the homeless makes a simple, clear, and effective statement about the financial value that Common Ground is creating.

These figures, says founder Rosanne Haggerty, impress donors and policymakers. "The economic argument moves you out of a partisan discussion very quickly. It's clear that society will be spending money on homelessness, and it is wiser to get good results for people and communities." In fact, continues Haggerty, "The success of supportive housing, tracking the data on cost savings, resulted in Mayor Michael Bloomberg and Governor George Pataki signing a ten-year agreement in 2004 to shift funds away from higher-cost systems into supportive housing targeted at the chronic homeless."

Haggerty gets right to the heart of the matter for policy-makers and taxpayers alike: If we're going to spend money for social benefits, why not spend it wisely? And to spend money wisely, we need to know the economic value we're creating with those social benefits.

Government and private funding organizations are beginning to understand this concept. They are becoming more engaged in ensuring that their investments lead to good performance. When a funder is deciding whether to invest in a specific area, the key determinant is still strategic fit with policy objectives or mission. However, because of the increasing stress on government budgets and philanthropic giving, more scrutiny is being given to economic analysis of a nonprofit's efficiency and effectiveness as determined by objective analysis.

I've seen this trend while serving on the board of the Greater Twin Cities United Way, a major funder of nonprofit social services in the Minneapolis–St. Paul area. United Way began to shift its focus toward economic value in 2009. Individual and corporate donations that the organization needed to invest in human services weren't sufficient to keep up with the community's needs. So United Way began analyzing the return on investment (ROI) that it receives from the investment it makes in workforce development agencies it funds by comparing the investment it makes to the economic benefit created by those agencies from their social interventions. It intends to follow suit in other areas.

Other organizations as well are studying the approach of comparing investment made to economic value created from social benefit. Units of government are introducing legislation specifically calling for pay-for-performance contracting between municipalities and service providers. These contracts require measuring outcomes, capturing the economic benefits those outcomes create, and rewarding organizations that can deliver superior results. My expectation is that these types of analysis and payment systems will increasingly be adopted by states, the federal government, and other units of government.

Nonprofits need to get ahead of these trends in order to stay economically viable and seek growth capital. They need to focus on both the social outcomes they create and how those outcomes translate into dollars and cents.

Such analysis also helps funding organizations work with their constituencies. Many funders are under pressure to show results within a time frame that is much too short considering the size of the problems that they're trying to address. State legislatures function within a two-year election cycle. For-profit companies and their related philanthropies budget annually. Establishing an economic value for nonprofit services gives government and philanthropists the data they need to justify to their stakeholders their decision to support an organization.

I am by no means suggesting that society should evaluate nonprofits solely on the basis of financial return. I am proposing that we recognize the monetary value of social benefit and use that value as a way to measure, capture, and reward the social performance of organizations. We can even use that analysis to provide long-term growth capital to nonprofits— capital that could enable the best organizations to grow to a size where they can effectively address the huge social problems we face.

CARINGBRIDGE: ESTABLISHING VALUE

CaringBridge uses one simple and effective model for establishing the economic value of a social benefit: beneficiaries donate in response to the value they perceive they have received. Although CaringBridge is a nonprofit, its business model bears a close resemblance to that of a for-profit: customers and users provide financial support for the direct service they receive.

CaringBridge enables people to create personal Web sites to connect with their community through times of ill health. The organization provides its service for free, but it solicits donations from everyone who uses one of its sites. It receives at least one donation from users of 72 percent of its sites. The donations aren't particularly large; they average sixty-eight dollars each, and many people donate just once. Nevertheless, these donations not only cover costs but build a surplus that CaringBridge uses to keep current technologically, reach more partner organizations that recommend the site to patients, and do all the other things it needs to do to serve more people.

Having beneficiaries determine the economic value works for CaringBridge because it exceeds its operating costs. This is an effective way to raise money because it would be difficult, if not impossible, for CaringBridge to place a dollar value on its outcome—the sense of community and support experienced by the people who come together at a CaringBridge Web site.

CaringBridge's model certainly wouldn't work for every organization. In the case of CaringBridge, there's a direct link of value between users (many of whom have the resources to make a donation) and the services. A nursing home might be able to function this way. Higher education institutions certainly use something close to this model when they solicit gifts from alumni. But this model would not work where the user, participant, or consumer is not the primary economic beneficiary or simply doesn't have the money to donate—like RISE! and other antipoverty programs.

CALCULATING THE ECONOMIC VALUE OF SOCIAL BENEFITS

Quality nonprofits create benefits to society by addressing social problems, and virtually all the social benefits they create have monetary or economic value that can be identified and measured. A nonprofit that calculates this value can leverage its success into more effective fundraising, revenue generation, pay-for-performance relationships, and better ways of capitalizing growth.

An organization creates economic value when it increases revenue or eliminates costs, or both, for a stakeholder. These benefits typically accrue over time. The three components—increased revenue, decreased cost, and time—hold true whether the organization operates as a for-profit or a nonprofit.

Notice that the organization's costs don't enter into the equation. Costs and revenue are, of course, vitally important to the long-term health of any organization, but no one is going to pay any nonprofit for reducing its costs. You are (or you should be) paid for the value you create for others—through your outcomes, not your inputs or outputs. I emphasize this point because government and philanthropic funders typically evaluate nonprofits by focusing on their costs instead of the economic benefit or ROI they generate. More than once I've been asked why RISE!'s costs are higher than another program's, even when our ROI is higher than that program's.

Think of buying a car. As a consumer, do you care what it cost General Motors to build your vehicle? Or are you more focused on its value to you? General Motors cares about the cost because if its costs are higher than its revenue, the company isn't profitable. GM also wants to know what the car is worth to you, its customer, because that value translates directly into the price it can charge you for the benefit of owning the car. As long as the benefit price is sufficiently higher than its cost, GM has enough margin to continue operating profitably. As the customer, however, you are concerned only with the price you pay for the value you receive.

Virtually every effective nonprofit creates economic value. However, there are some vitally important organizations—like art museums, zoos, and orchestras—where the economic value would be extraordinarily difficult, perhaps impossible, to establish. Of course, these organizations are essential to the community's quality of life and have an intrinsic value. But they also create jobs and contribute to the economy in many ways. How do you determine the specific cash value they generate for state government or some other entity? In these cases, the economic value equation is not a useful tool for management. Management's time and energy are better spent in pursuing other ways to build a financially stable organization.

However, every other nonprofit should be interested in establishing the economic value of its outcomes, because when its outcomes increase revenue or eliminate costs for a stakeholder, that economic value becomes a powerful tool.

Benefits that accrue in the future are worth money in the present. When someone gets and keeps a living-wage job, when an ex-felon stays out of jail, when an addict stays clean for a number of years, when a fragile senior is able to live independently rather than in a nursing home—all of these events have financial benefits now and in a foreseeable future. To accurately establish the economic value of programs that have outcomes like these, you must capture the value of these future benefits and compare them to their costs.

When you want to know what future cash flows are worth to you right now, the tool that is commonly used is net present value analysis (NPV). Economists, accountants, investors, and business analysts use it in capital budgeting to determine whether an investment is worth making financially. If the future cash inflows exceed the future cash outflows, discounted for the time in the future when they occur, the investment is considered financially sound. Discounting is a way of quantifying the time value of money (the idea that money available now is worth more than the same amount of money available in the future because it could be earning interest) and the risk or uncertainty of the anticipated future cash flows (which might be less than expected).[1]

Another extremely important tool for determining the soundness of an investment or for comparing alternative investments is ROI. ROI is calculated by dividing the cost of the investment into the benefit or gain less the cost of the investment:

ROI = Gain – cost of investment/cost of investment

Business leaders use ROI and NPV to evaluate potential investments like developing a new product, acquiring a business, building a new plant, and purchasing new equipment. The social service sector should be using financial tools in the same ways for a number of reasons:

- Government can determine which programs provide the best social and economic return to society and therefore which ones it should invest in.

- Social investors and donors can identify those organizations that provide the best returns to society and use that information as part of their decision making.

- Nonprofit managers and boards of directors can make better decisions about how to spend limited resources. Nonprofits can use NPV analysis to assess the feasibility of investing in a new program or the economic soundness of an existing one and to convince stakeholders (including donors and government supporters) of the economic value that their programming generates in addition to its social value.

- Social entrepreneurs can be motivated to found organizations that serve populations who have greater barriers to success, like the generational poor. Certainly we should help people who have temporarily fallen on hard times, but those who live within chronic poverty generally cost the government more in subsidies and tax receipts over a longer period of time than those in situational poverty. Therefore, the high economic value of their maintaining living-wage jobs or using many fewer public subsidies is worthy of attention and remuneration.

Only when the social services sector addresses the specific economic value of social benefits can we become truly effective at addressing the huge social problems of our day.

ESTABLISHING ECONOMIC VALUE AT RISE!

Here's how RISE! established the economic value of its benefits to state government, which led to the pay-for-performance relationship that partially funds our work.

RISE!'s goal is for participants to get and keep a good job for at least two years. When we achieve that goal, participants and their families obviously benefit financially. But so do local, state, and federal governments. Those who earn a living wage with benefits are paying taxes to the government rather than receiving subsidies from it. Their family has health insurance, which means family members are less likely to use the emergency room for expensive primary care. They are less likely to commit acts that put them back into the criminal justice system. The state isn't paying for low-income child care.

We were able to demonstrate this return to society in 1995 with the help of a formula developed by Art Rolnick, then director of research at the Minneapolis Federal Reserve Bank, and with economic analysis done by state of Minnesota economists. Here's how it works. For each person who climbs from $10,000 to $20,000 on the income ladder, Minnesota state analysts calculated an average annual benefit to the state of

$3,800. They calculated the present value (PV) of these benefits over the next fifteen years to be $31,000. (Fifteen was chosen as a conservative estimate of the number of years a RISE! graduate would work.) To keep the model conservative, they used a discount rate of 9 percent, which at the time was twice the state's cost of funds.[2]

That analysis paved the way for the pay-for-performance contract RISE! has with the state. When one of our graduates is placed in a job at least $10,000 greater in income than when he or she entered our program, we earn one-half of a performance payment. If that person remains in that job or a better one for a year, the state pays us the other half. The total amount of the two payments is $18,000. (The NPV was calculated at $13,000 [$31,000–$18,000].)

Our actual results have been better than projected. Our graduates have averaged an increase in earnings of more than $15,000, or 50 percent better than the $10,000 the state anticipated. Based on our track record since 1997, RISE! creates a total PV to the state of $50,000 per successful graduate rather than $31,000 as predicted. The state pays us $18,000, less than half the $50,000 value we generate. And for every dollar the state has paid us since 1997, the year the pay-for-performance statute went into effect, the state has received $7.24. That's a 624 percent ROI.

Note that the state pays RISE! only for its successful graduates. That's our risk and reward under the agreement. Our pay-for-performance contract with the state is based on a statute that received bipartisan support in the Minnesota legislature. Democrats liked our approach because it invested in the people who are hardest to employ. Republicans supported it because of the model's provisions for strict accountability.

If RISE! had initially asked the state to support a program that serves ex-felons based solely on the social benefit, we would have gotten nowhere. There isn't a lot of political interest in supporting this population versus, say, displaced youth or dislocated workers. Ex-felons don't have a strong lobbying presence in the capitol. But we had outcomes data and a sound economic model that established financial benefits. We could demonstrate to the legislature that supporting our work made indisputable financial sense, not just social sense. As Rosanne Haggerty of Common Ground points out, financial tools take the discussion out of the realm of whose participants are more worthy and into the realm of straightforward decision making about where to invest resources.

BUILDING RELIABLE SOURCES OF CAPITAL FOR NONPROFITS AND SOCIAL ENTERPRISES

Once we start thinking about the social contribution that nonprofits and social enterprises make in terms of economic value, we can take an entirely fresh look at the size and scope of these organizations and how we finance them. Given what we've learned in the business world about the effectiveness of using large-scale, well-financed operations to attack large-scale problems, our current approach doesn't make sense.

We have continuing, expensive social problems in the United States: poverty, teen pregnancy, the cost of incarcerating prisoners who reoffend, low-achieving schools, and the runaway costs of medical care, to name just a few. The need for solutions to these problems is high. Yet we are trying to meet that need with organizations that for the most part are small compared to the problems they tackle. There are hundreds of thousands of nonprofits with less than $5 million in revenue. Even the most successful nonprofits, like Goodwill Industries and Habitat for Humanity, have revenues the size of middle-sized businesses. A major factor is the lack of capital needed to scale up and sustain the organization at scale. Nonprofits understand this and are looking to do something about it. Many of the organizations profiled in this book, including College Summit, Playworks, and Common Ground, are engaged in major growth initiatives.

If these nonprofits were traditional for-profit businesses, they would obtain outside capital by selling stock or issuing long-term debt such as bonds. They would use this capital to build additional capacity, fund long-term research and development, expand to other markets, and make other long-range investments that would create social and economic value. But they aren't for-profit businesses, and these traditional nonprofits typically receive funding from federal and state grants, supplemented by philanthropy. The organization is usually required to spend the funding in one to two years. As a result, nonprofits often have to make longer-term investments out of their annual expense budgets, or else they ramp up capital campaigns from time to time to seek philanthropic support.

Nonprofits don't have the same access to long-term capital that for-profits do. Why not?

Social venture capital exists, of course. Some is invested in organizations to expand proven concepts; some is invested in start-ups. But there is virtually nothing available to sustain nonprofits at a scale commensurate with the need. That's because there aren't enough social investors with sufficient investment capital to make a difference. Social capital amounts to hundreds of millions of dollars spread thin across a dizzying array of projects, while market rate capital, typically focused on for-profit business, adds up to trillions of dollars.

Like for-profit businesses, nonprofits need a full array of sustainable vehicles that provide market rate capital to grow. So what to do? First, nonprofits must measure outcomes and establish the economic value of those outcomes. Then they need to turn to the same financial tools like NPV and ROI that for-profits use to attract capital for growth.

Multiple organizations are exploring ways to create sustainable funding for social purpose organizations. Three innovative programs (two of them in the pilot stage) that I'll discuss are Lumni's mutual-fund-like investment pools that fund higher education for low-income students in four countries; social impact bonds that are funding programs to reduce recidivism among prisoners in Great Britain; and the human capital performance bond to fund high-performing human service providers in Minnesota.

As you consider these financing tools, think about a continuum of social-purpose funding in terms of ROI as shown in Figure 6.1. The continuum progresses from left to right as follows:

- *No financial return expected.* This covers philanthropy and traditional government appropriations.

- *Below-market return expected.* Investors expect a return, albeit one that is less than they would receive through

Figure 6.1 Continuum of Social-Purpose Funding

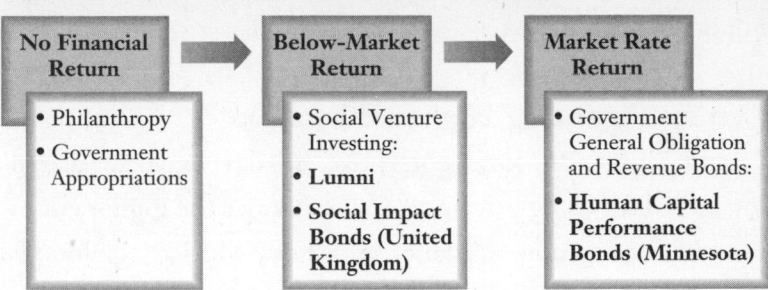

traditional commercial investments. This covers what is known as social investing. Those who invest in this category are willing to accept a lower return because of the social good it is creating. These funders can include foundations, social investment mutual funds, and wealthy individuals. Lumni's mutual fund–like investment pools and the social impact bond fall into this category.

- *Market rate return expected.* Investors are expecting a return equal to that which they can obtain in the commercial world. A market rate return makes this investment vehicle highly attractive to investors, including banks, insurance companies, and pension funds. Examples include municipal bonds like general obligation bonds and revenue bonds.[3] Human capital performance bonds represent an attractive innovation to social investors who can receive both a market rate return and meet their social interests.

Only when social-purpose investments offer returns comparable to those that investors can achieve from other market rate investments will we have sufficient capital available for nonprofits to thrive.

Lumni: Financing Higher Education

Lumni, a for-profit social enterprise, has developed an intriguing model for using private capital to finance the higher education of low-income students in Chile, Mexico, Colombia, and the United States. Lumni does not give out student loans. Rather, the enterprise develops and manages social investment funds, raising money from groups like angel investors, impact funds, the Inter-American Development Bank, foundations, universities, and wealthy donors. It selects the students who will receive these funds based on their potential and commitment to succeed in higher education and their chosen career path.

Once the students have graduated, they are committed, under a contract that they signed when they accepted the funds, to paying Lumni a fixed percentage of their income for a fixed number of months, between 40 and 120 months. The payment is generally between 4 and 8 percent, but never more than 15 percent. Paying a percentage of income reduces the risk to students and their families. A person with no income makes no payments during the time of his or her unemployment. A person whose income is lower than expected pays only the fixed percentage of that income.

Lumni offers investors multiple funds with different purposes. In Colombia, there are funds to finance former combatants and refugees. In Mexico, funds are used to provide financing to the physically challenged and those who will be attending top international universities, like Harvard, MIT, and the London School of Economics. In Chile, there's a fund to finance the education of those who plan to teach in rural areas.

Lumni's investors receive either a market rate or below-market return depending on the fund that they invest in. They are content with that because Lumni is fulfilling a social purpose that they believe in. That is one reason Lumni establishes different funds, each with a focused social agenda.

Lumni's staff have the job of predicting ROI, given the cost of education in a particular career and the income potential of a given person in a given field in a particular country. It's a highly sophisticated analysis, but no more so than the assessment of risk and reward that banks and insurance companies perform. Lumni's goal is to demonstrate the profit-making potential of this human capital financing so that traditional financing institutions will find it attractive. As of August 2011, funds had reached approximately $25 million, allowing Lumni to invest in 2,300 students from four countries. At that point, 125 students who had received funding from Lumni had graduated, with many more close to graduation. Some had become investors themselves in addition to making their contractual payments.

With 125 graduated students so far and between 40 months and 120 months of payments to make, it's too soon to know if Lumni will be achieving the financial returns it is targeting; however, it believes that it is on goal. Still, this work provides an exciting new approach to financing the development of human capital—in this case, high-potential, low-income students who otherwise would not be able to continue their education.

The Social Impact Bond:
Reducing Recidivism in England

In 2010, a pilot program for the first social impact bond was officially launched by Social Finance, a London-based social investment organization that is working with the United Kingdom's Ministry of Justice on this project. Social Finance was founded in 2007 for the purpose of developing an effective social investment market in the United Kingdom. According to Social Finance, the need for new ways to capitalize social enterprise in the United Kingdom is very similar to ours in the United States:

> The UK's social sector—which comprises charities and organizations with a social purpose as well as nonprofit and for-profit social enterprises—is currently held back by a chronic lack of investment capital. Traditionally, available finance has tended to fall at either of two extremes: 100% subsidy grants or fully commercial loans. Social Finance aims to connect the social sector to the capital markets, thereby ensuring access to a full range of financial instruments.[4]

The purpose of this social impact bond pilot is twofold: to reduce reoffending rates among short-sentence male prisoners leaving Peterborough Prison by at least 7.5 percent and to "develop a new asset class that aligns social and financial returns and brings in new capital to address social programs."[5]

Criminal offenders who reoffend cost the British government serious money. According to Social Finance, over forty thousand adults leave prison each year after serving sentences of less than a year. Housing these prisoners costs hundreds of millions of dollars annually. When they leave prison, they typically receive little or no formal support to help them reintegrate into society, and nearly three-quarters reoffend within two years. For former prisoners under age twenty-one, the rate of recidivism is even higher: over 90 percent.[6]

Here's how the social impact bond works.

Social Finance has raised a fund of 5 million pounds sterling from foundations, charitable trusts, and other organizations interested in social investment. It then manages the fund and uses the money to provide capital to social services providers with a track record of reducing recidivism. These providers work with three thousand prisoners during incarceration at and after release from Peterborough Prison over a six-year period.

Former prisoners who become productive members of society rather than reoffending save money for the government's criminal justice system and increase government revenue when they pay taxes. If the rate of reoffending among this group from Peterborough Prison is reduced by 7.5 percent or more below the previous rate of recidivism, the government pays investors a share of the long-term savings. Once that threshold of 7.5 percent is reached, the return to investors increases as the success of the program increases (the rate of recidivism goes down). Investors can realize up to a maximum of 13 percent return.

If the pilot program does not achieve at least 7.5 percent reduction in reoffending, the government pays nothing, and investors receive nothing. Should that happen, it's likely the pilot would be discontinued.

The social impact bond is a hybrid means of generating capital. Although it's called a bond, it behaves less like a bond and more like a social venture capital investment.[7] Like a bond, it has an upper limit on returns—13 percent. But like venture capital, the amount of return is tied to performance. Also like venture capital, the investor takes all the risk and enjoys much of the reward of success, albeit at below-market rates. Thirteen percent is approximately half of what market rate venture capital might require. Social Finance's goal is to develop "a new asset class that aligns social and financial returns and brings in new capital to address social problems."[8] The Peterborough Prison pilot program is a first step in accomplishing that.

Social impact bonds have captured the imagination of many outside the United Kingdom. They are currently being analyzed for their application to the U.S. marketplace and elsewhere. One concern of investigators is the scale-up potential of these bonds if they do work, because for this kind of below-market social venture capital, availability is limited and it is expensive to organize into investment pools.

As of this writing, it's too early to see results. But Social Finance has identified and researched other potential applications for this type of capitalization: reducing the number of children who are excluded from mainstream classes and receive some form of special education; increasing support for the people who provide foster care to children, since foster care costs the government much less than residential placement for children; and reducing acute hospital stays by increasing community-based health care. In all of these cases, the government is a direct beneficiary of a social good. And the economic value of that social good can be quantified.

Human Capital Performance Bonds: Minnesota's Pilot

In order to obtain adequate capital to scale up and truly address our daunting social problems, we need financial instruments that provide market rate returns to those who invest in social purpose organizations. That's what we're developing with the human capital performance bond (HUCAP) in Minnesota. We speak of human capital to express that this financial instrument invests in people. The word *performance* is part of the name because the funds that the bond provides are available only to organizations that demonstrate their performance in terms of measurable, quantifiable outcomes, evaluated by ROI.

In Minnesota, as in the rest of the United States, there are too few resources to finance nonprofits that achieve measurable outcomes with economic value. In fact, as health care costs continue to outstrip state revenues over the next twenty-five years, much social service spending will be squeezed out of state budgets. This is not primarily a function of the economy, but rather a result of the aging population and the increased use and cost of health care. A group of social entrepreneurs, nonprofit leaders, economists, policy analysts, and advocates are developing the HUCAP, a market rate, AA state bond that will fund nonprofits in a way similar to the way states fund a bridge, tunnel, or stadium.[9]

The bill establishing a $10 million pilot project for the HUCAP became law in July 2011. It was endorsed by more than seventy organizations, including economists, underwriters, business leaders, nonprofit and foundation executives, civic officials, and thought leaders representing every political viewpoint. The basic mechanism of the HUCAP is simple: if the social outcomes that a nonprofit generates create economic value that is greater than the state's cost of borrowing the funds, then the state will have both a social and economic incentive to sell the bonds.

With the HUCAP, the relationship among investors, government, and nonprofits is somewhat different than with the social impact bond. Here's how it works (Figure 6.2):

- The state sets economic criteria that qualify nonprofits to participate. The criteria are based on measurable outcomes that generate revenue or decrease costs for the state—outcomes that generate an ROI above the state's cost of borrowing and administering the bond. For example, as workforce programs increase participants' incomes, economic value, including cash, is created for government.

- Investors buy these bonds from the state based on their assessment of risk and return, just as they would with any other bond.

- The state deposits the invested funds in a performance pool, and the money is held and invested until the payout terms are met.

Figure 6.2   Human Capital Performance Bond

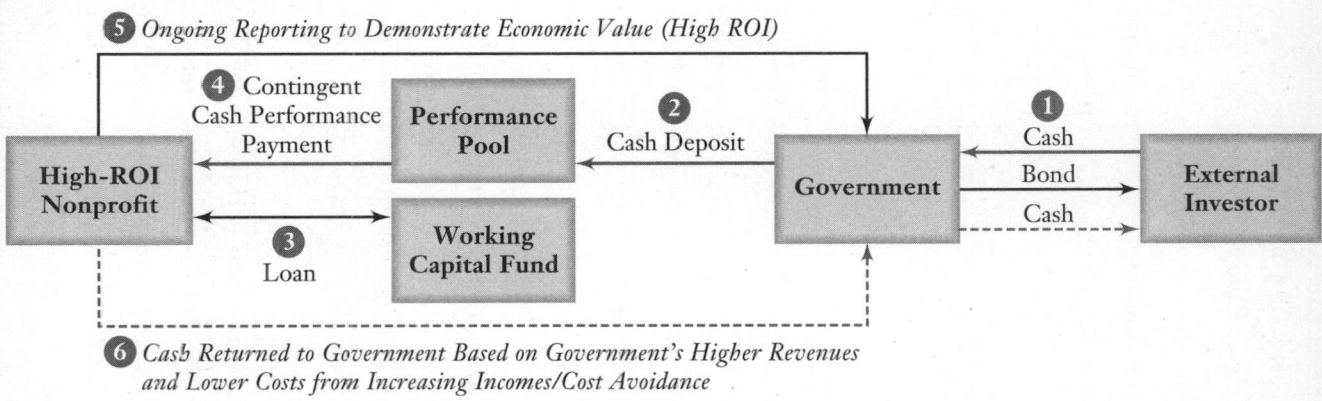

5 *Ongoing Reporting to Demonstrate Economic Value (High ROI)*

4 Contingent Cash Performance Payment

Performance Pool

2 Cash Deposit

High-ROI Nonprofit

3 Loan

Working Capital Fund

Government

1 Cash

Bond

Cash

External Investor

6 *Cash Returned to Government Based on Government's Higher Revenues and Lower Costs from Increasing Incomes/Cost Avoidance*

① External investor buys state Appropriation bond that is linked to specific economic criteria established by government; structured as normal, market rate of return.

② State deposits investor funds in performance pool where it's held until payout terms are met by pre-certified nonprofit.

③ Nonprofit qualifies for working capital loan from working capital fund.

④ Performance pool pays out to nonprofit based on nonprofit meeting government performance goals.

⑤ Oversight board annually validates performance value (ROI) to state.

⑥ If performance targets are met, government receives high ROI and cash flow to fund principal repayment, interest, and administrative costs. If performance targets are not met, state has use of funds for principal repayment, interest, or other purposes until bond period terminates.

Structure term ends at end of bond term. Alternatively, performance pool continues operating, funded by cash returns reinvested by government.

- Participating nonprofits qualify for low-cost working capital loans that are provided by foundation program-related investments (PRIs) and bank community development corporations (CDCs).

- Once nonprofits achieve an outcome, the performance pool provides a payment based on the NPV of the benefit being created.

- Economic benefit to the state begins at the same time that the state pays the nonprofit from the pool.

- The state books (that is, captures the benefit in a separate account) the incremental taxes and savings in public costs by debiting state department budgets that have benefited.

- The state pays bond interest and amortizes principal to the bondholder from these captured cash benefits.

- If performance targets are met, (1) the nonprofits receive investment to expand their programs, (2) investors receive the market rate return they were promised at the time the bond was issued, and (3) the state receives a high ROI that generates cash flow to fund interest and principal repayment, and, perhaps incremental cash to reinvest in the pool.

- If performance targets are not met, (1) the nonprofits do not receive funds, (2) but investors receive the return they were promised when the bond was issued, and (3) the state has use of the funds for principal repayment, interest, retiring the bond early, or other purposes until the bond period terminates.

Human capital performance bonds are somewhat riskier than the most highly rated municipal bonds, general obligation bonds, which are issued by states exclusively for buildings and equipment. These bonds are legally a debt of the state. Human capital performance bonds are annual appropriation bonds. Payment of annual appropriation bonds is not legal debt. Technically the state could choose not to pay investors. In practice, however, they don't do that, since the agencies that rate them would downgrade the rating on their other bonds. The ratings downgrade would in turn push up the interest that the state is legally obligated to pay on all its other bonds—an expensive trade-off.

Another way the HUCAP bond is different from other bonds is that the cash flow created by the nonprofit's performance will pay the debt service without costing the taxpayer (the general fund of the state) anything. Indeed, if the returns are higher than the state's cost of debt, there will be positive arbitrage (incremental cash benefit) to the state. In this way, the nonprofits pay the total cost of the investment without any cost and little risk to the state.

Supporters assert that the HUCAPs have the potential to be a major redesign idea affecting much of state government by providing incremental investment spending for cash-starved human services where appropriations are not and will not be sufficient in the foreseeable future. Detractors argue that human services should be paid out of appropriations only and that the state should not borrow for operating purposes, even for incremental investments. They believe that it is the obligation of taxpayers, rather than investors, to pay for services the state deems important. Others think that the state shouldn't borrow for operations since that increases the risk to the state. Still others are concerned that it will give an excuse to people who want to cut taxes and cut the budget to replace appropriations with bonding.

Many believe, as do I, that we need to try new approaches for generating incremental revenue for human services that supplement current appropriations and philanthropy. HUCAPs are the only concept we now have to accomplish that goal on a sufficient scale to make a difference.

The only way to determine if the concerns expressed are real and if the benefits prove out is to pilot the concept. Unintended consequences and opportunities can't be determined any way other than a real-world experiment.

THE IMPORTANCE OF MARKET RATE INVESTMENT

We need to continue working toward developing market rate investment vehicles that can provide capital to any social issue where social benefit can be monetized and where the economic value created is equal to or greater than the cost of capital to the entity providing the capital. The economic value of some social benefits is well established. College graduation, for example, leads to higher wages and lower unemployment. We know that the state saves money when we can provide health care services to fragile seniors who remain in a relative's home or other less costly alternatives than a nursing home. In England, Social Finance talks about reducing the need for residential placement for children by developing better support systems for adults who provide foster care. The data on these benefits exist and are readily available.

I want to be clear. The financial models that are currently available to nonprofits (social venture capital and PRIs, for example) play an important role. We need to continue using them; indeed, we should be using them more widely. But by themselves they are not sufficient to build organizations of the scale needed to address our daunting social problems.

We can lay the foundation for developing organizations of the size, scale, and effectiveness we need by doing the necessary analysis to establish the economic value of social good. We need to create new ways to do so. These organizations need funding that is reliable and sustainable, and the best way to create that funding is to develop market rate instruments that attract new investors with ample capital. This is something we must do. The cost of not addressing our social problems effectively is too high in terms of financial strain on our limited resources and, more important, in human lives.

QUESTIONS TO HELP YOUR ORGANIZATION CREATE ECONOMIC VALUE FROM SOCIAL BENEFIT

- In what ways does your organization create economic value? Do you produce products or services that have monetary value to you and your stakeholders? Do you make it possible for stakeholders to significantly cut expenses or increase revenues?
- Do you measure bottom-line outcomes that quantify your social benefit to those stakeholders who benefit economically?
- Have you monetized the benefit that government receives— in terms of increased revenues (taxes paid) and lower

public subsidies and costs—as a result of your social actions?

- Can you benefit from creating a pay-for-performance contract with these stakeholders?
- Do you know the ROI that your organization creates for government?

7

Principle #7

Be Learning Driven

The best-laid plans change frequently—not because of poor research or planning but because life refuses to behave in a predictable fashion. Reality tests our assumptions and reveals surprising flaws. We implement our decisions and find they have unintended consequences. Variables over which we have no control—from natural disasters, to the health of the economy, to who walks in the door—shift in unanticipated ways.

We can't predict the future, but we must be prepared to learn from it. Successful organizations—and individuals—accept this fact of life, learning and adapting over and over again. A thriving organization in its tenth year may look very different from the way it did when it started. Successful organizations succeed by being persistently learning driven.

GRAMEEN BANK: LEARNING TO BE FLEXIBLE

Grameen Bank is a prime example of an organization that was faced with the unexpected and used the situation to learn and adapt, in the process transforming itself into a stronger and more effective organization.

In 1998, about twenty-five years after Grameen Bank began making microloans in Bangladesh, its much-prized repayment rate started slipping badly. According to founder Muhammad Yunus, the difficulties had begun in 1995.[1] Egged on by political forces in Bangladesh, Yunus says, husbands of many members demanded that their wives stop going to meetings and paying their loan installments until the bank changed its group tax policy. Under this policy, each member belonged to a small group, and all of its members provided motivation and support and helped keep each other accountable for payments. The policy decreed that a percentage of each member's loan amount be deposited in a group savings account. This money was deposited in a group fund, from which members could take additional loans if everyone in their group agreed.[2] Grameen Bank did resolve the group tax issue, but many members continued to stay away.

Then came the worst of disasters in a country riddled with natural disasters: a flood that covered half the country for ten weeks. Many Bangladeshis lost all of their possessions, including their homes. Grameen Bank issued fresh loans for rehabilitating houses and restarting businesses, but the repayment policies were too onerous for many. Once again, members began dropping out.

When the situation did not improve by itself, the organization went back to the drawing board. The purpose of lifting people out of poverty was as strong as ever. But it was clearly time to review the experience and see what they could learn from it.

The original Grameen Bank had standardized policies and procedures with no exceptions allowed. This franchise-like standardization had enabled it to scale up from branches in one village in 1973 to branches in thousands of villages in 2000. The flood had revealed ways in which this rigidity no longer served well—particularly in providing a practical path for someone in default to get back on track. Grameen's philosophy is that the poor will always repay if the systems are designed correctly. It was clearly time to get creative.

Grameen pilot-tested new policies and procedures in a few branches, reworked them, went through the cycle again, and began releasing a comprehensive, redesigned business model in 2001. There were so many changes that the bank thought of itself as a transformed organization and called itself Grameen II. The conversion involved developing systems and infrastructure to convert millions of microloans to the new model. This change required training 12,000 staff members in 1,175 branches.

Grameen II gave branch staff much more flexibility. They could now customize the size and length of the loan to the individual borrower's needs, within certain parameters. Borrowers who ran into unexpected trouble could now refinance their basic loan, negotiating new terms to give them time to respond to whatever event had sidetracked them. This provided borrowers with a much-needed alternative to defaulting and dropping out of the system entirely. They could remain, as Yunus put it, "a valued client." This also took stress off the branch staff and the members of each borrowers' group since they are no longer expected to pressure the nonpaying borrower to resume her original payment schedule.

The new model abolished the group savings fund with its group tax. Each member is still required to save, but individually, so that anything a member saves is available for her own use only. Other innovations include a pension fund, higher education loans, housing loans, and loan insurance. There are special programs for Gold Members (those who maintain a 100 percent repayment record for seven years) and special programs for destitute members. And finally the Five Star Branch program awards one of five different colored stars to a branch for meeting certain criteria on the way to lifting all its members out of poverty.

What began with a natural disaster and a crisis in accountability has resulted in a stronger, more flexible business model for Grameen Bank. The flood, as Grameen's leadership saw it, amplified existing problems and provided an opportunity to learn what was needed to solve those problems. Grameen identified the policies that had created obstacles for members' success. Its leaders took the time to figure out why these policies were not working as intended. They developed solutions and piloted them on a small scale. Then they took the best solutions and rolled them out over a period of time, while ensuring that the necessary organization-wide systems were put into place to support the changes at the branch level. The result of this thoughtful, learning-driven process was what author Alex Counts calls "a quantum leap" and a "break-through" in being responsive "to the needs of the poor."[3]

BUILDING AN ENDURING LEARNING CULTURE

Learning shouldn't be something that happens only when events force the issue. Throughout this chapter, indeed throughout this book, I am advocating for learning through experience and for making that learning an integral and routine part of your organization's culture and therefore the way that you conduct business. Regardless of whether you're a start-up or a well-established organization, it's important to create and reinforce a culture focused on learning.

How you operationalize the principle of being learning driven will depend to some extent on the stage of development of your enterprise. For an innovative start-up, one of the biggest barriers to experiential learning is, interestingly, over-planning. Of course, you need to gather the best and most relevant information and then create a well-reasoned plan. Planning is invaluable. It provides a clearly conceived launching pad and teaches you a great deal that you can use no matter how events unfold. But too much planning can delay your start-up, hamper your ability to learn through experience, and ultimately get in the way of fulfilling your mission. There is no substitute for actually working with participants. Only then can you evaluate, reflect, and adapt.

Michael Patton, former chairman of the American Evaluation Association, who worked with RISE! during its formative years, describes overplanning as trying to hit your target by shouting, "Ready, aim, aim, aim, aim." What you really want, Patton says, is "Fire, learn, aim. Fire, learn, aim." There comes a time when you need to "just do it," always bearing in mind that you'll need to make necessary adjustments quickly.

In addition, too much focus on a specific plan can give your organization tunnel vision. You can execute an excellent plan brilliantly but still not achieve the desired results. Too much focus on the plan itself can obscure a critical underlying issue. Or, most likely, the world may simply change between the plan's conception and your implementation, however short a period of time that is.

Overplanning can take place at any stage of an organization's development. But a more common hindrance to learning in a mature organization is becoming stuck in your ways so you don't see opportunities to learn and grow. Successful organizations don't wait for a crisis or disaster to get them unstuck; they create a culture of learning and institutionalize ongoing processes for gathering information internally and externally. Their strategic and tactical decisions are simply better because they understand their performance, their results, and the world they operate in.

At RISE! we found two methods of intelligence harvesting to be a powerful combination:

- Regular internal lessons-learned sessions for the staff
- Formal research and evaluation

We recommend setting aside a regular time for staff to reflect and evaluate. By holding these lessons-learned sessions quarterly, you demonstrate in a formal way the organization's commitment to the principle of being learning driven. Lessons-learned sessions last about three hours and should be led by a professional outside facilitator until someone in your organization has developed the necessary skills. The facilitator should be trained to elicit relevant information in a positive way, deal with any issues that interfere with obtaining the best information, and help the group come up with potential solutions. All staff participate. After each session, you issue a lessons-learned report to summarize information gathered, decisions made, and any actions steps with the responsible person identified.

Whatever the mechanics of your process, lessons-learned sessions should enable you and staff members to:

- Examine every aspect of the operation as needed
- Think through problems
- Share all ideas and points of view
- Confront and deal with conflicts
- Evaluate what is learned
- Apply those lessons to improving programming and operations

The process you use for lessons-learned sessions, should, of course, be subject to learning and improvement.

The underlying message of these sessions is that when things don't work as expected, they should not be dismissed or swept under the nearest rug. Rather, they should be examined and evaluated so that the organization can learn from them and improve. An empowered organization does this with a sense of personal accountability to fix mistakes and pursue opportunities.

Our second method of intelligence harvesting is formal research and evaluation. Most traditional nonprofits have a grant writer on staff whose job is to write accountability reports to funders. But an emphasis on results requires ongoing intelligence on how well we're meeting our expectations: where we are meeting our goals, where we are falling short, and anything else the data can tell us about what's working and what isn't. RISE! therefore hired a part-time researcher with a master's degree in research and evaluation to provide the information we need to be learning driven, as well as any evaluation reports our funders require.

You need research to provide the information that drives your results. Once you identify something that is a problem (for example, too many people dropping out of your program), you dig deeper, asking a number of questions—for example:

- Who is dropping out at the greatest rate?
- Are there demographic similarities among the dropouts?
- Does dropping out have to do with the number of barriers the participant is dealing with?
- At what point in the program are people dropping out?

Research can also discover the best practices that other organizations employ or possible solutions to consider.

Research can tell you where you have a problem and how much of a problem it is, but it doesn't necessarily reveal how to fix it. For that you need lessons-learned sessions, discussions with staff, discussions with outsiders, and a lot of creative thinking. In the case of dropouts, lessons-learned sessions, and interviews with participants help identify underlying issues in the problems that the data analysis depicted. For us, these issues included outside influence, family problems, difficulty dealing with everyday problem solving, and fundamental issues with individuals' beliefs about their worthiness. Our search for solutions to this constellation of factors led us to understand that our training needed a third component beyond skills training and remedial education: empowerment.

To accomplish your mission, you need the best intelligence you can gather about any obstacles that are hindering you. For that, you need quantitative analysis from the data you collect and qualitative information from your staff, your participants, other stakeholders, experts, and creative thinkers.

Being learning driven requires building a learning culture that persists throughout an organization's entire existence, not just at the time of start-up or when it is facing unusual hardship. A learning-driven culture happens not by accident or declaration but by deliberate integration of learning into day-to-day operations.

PLAYWORKS: LEARNING TO SCALE

All the nonprofit leaders I talked to agreed: one event that precipitates a spurt in organizational learning is taking the organization to scale. The business model that worked so well when you and your original team were involved in day-to-day operations often needs to be distilled as you expand nationally or internationally. Your purpose remains firm, but your mission and strategy are open to reevaluation. To be most effective in fulfilling your purpose, you often need to invest more resources in fewer priorities, and that can mean letting go of worthy activities. You learn what to keep and what to let go. And you learn that serving your purpose can require ruthless pruning of your own activities.

"Going to scale has been an intense exercise," agrees Jill Vialet, president of Playworks, an organization that provides public schools with coaches whose job is to integrate healthy, positive play into the school day. When Vialet founded Playworks in the 1990s in San Francisco's Bay Area, being local afforded the original group a certain luxury of running physical activities programs for older youth, kids who'd been incarcerated, and emotionally disturbed kids, in addition to kids who attend low-income elementary schools. "We were good at that. We were really appreciated. But when it came time to think about what it would take to go to scale, to be effective in rolling it out, we needed to pare down." Vialet speaks to the need to get all the functions of the enterprise—program delivery, human resources, information technology, finance, training, and the rest—focused toward one precise target.

Vialet's long-term vision is a national movement that changes the American system of education so that "every kid in America gets to play every day." She and her colleagues at Playworks decided that vision could best be served by refining their mission for now and investing their resources on one primary group, elementary schools with low-income students, so they focused their mission and language: "We came to understand that our core business is making recess great." The program has five components, but, says Vialet, "when we make decisions, we ask ourselves, Does it help us make sure that recess is everything it can be?"

To accomplish "big, hairy, audacious" goals, Vialet says, "You need to be superdisciplined," and in this way Playworks has been able to roll out services from one city to twenty-seven cities. It has learned the power of tightening focus from what it does well to what is most important for accomplishing its purpose. Its leaders have also learned that growth can mean loss—the loss of satisfying activities and the sadness of disappointing people who received services that Playworks is no longer providing. The next time its goes through a growth spurt, chances are it will have those lessons in mind.

LESSONS LEARNED AT RISE!

Learning from experience doesn't have to mean your own experience, though it often does. I hope that the example of Playworks and other organizations throughout this book will help make your learning process more efficient and less painful. To that end, here are a few things that RISE! learned along the way.

How the Failure of
Outsourced Teaching Led to Success

Any successful entrepreneur knows that failure is a great teacher. In our original model, the role of RISE! was to assess needs and then outsource teaching and training, with each participant's coach as the hub of his or her learning. The idea was that the coach would review a participant's assessment data, the needs of the current job market, and the participant's interests. Then the coach would arrange for classes and training that were, we knew, readily available in the community. We certainly didn't expect to teach in-house.

So we sent participants who had remedial education needs, which was virtually everybody, to public remedial education, and a lot of them disappeared. They dropped out of school, and sometimes out of our program altogether. We wondered if their IQs were too low, but we tested and refuted that possibility. So what was the problem?

A member of our staff suggested that traditional teaching methods might not match our participants' learning style. When teaching math, for example, traditional classroom instructors say, "One plus one equals two," and they write it on the blackboard. These auditory and visual styles of learning work well for many people, but when we tested our participants' learning styles, we found that nearly half of them were primarily kinesthetic, or physical, learners. They learn best when they can feel and manipulate an item. If you put two blocks in front of them, for instance, they quickly learn that one block plus one block equals two blocks. So we had been sending participants off to learn in ways that had failed them earlier in their lives. We were making them relive the experience of feeling stupid, incompetent, and frustrated. As children and teens, they hadn't cut it in the classroom, so they had been sent to special education. Many acted out and became behavior problems. Some went to jail. Many dropped out of school as soon as they could. We later learned that a high proportion of people in prisons (one study puts it at 80 percent) are kinesthetic learners.[4]

As a first step, we hired Sylvan Learning Systems to teach our participants in small groups, using methods that suited their specific learning needs. The results were impressive. In an average of eight weeks, participants improved by an entire grade level and a half in their basic math, reading, and writing skills. Then we hired some of those instructors to teach in-house, and we modified the curriculum to be more work relevant and adult oriented. We added occupational skills training internally as well, including courses in Microsoft Office, customer service, and shop math.

In a complete reversal of our original plan, we no longer outsource teaching, with the exception of some specialized occupational classes (we send participants to high-quality technical colleges for those). Our learning process went from recognizing the failure of our original plan, to discovering the reasons for failing, to implementing a successful strategy. We learned that we had to do most of the teaching in-house, so we could tailor the teaching methods to the needs of our population. And we learned that a failure—when we apply learning strategies to it—can ultimately lead to success.

When Selecting Applicants, the Best Assessment Is Real Life

When RISE! was in its early days, we had a fairly elaborate assessment process for selecting applicants. The training we were providing was expensive, so it made sense to select only applicants who had the highest potential to succeed. Assessment is also expensive, but the investment seemed worthwhile, since by weeding out potential dropouts up front, we reasoned, we would save money later.

With the assistance of assessment professionals we developed a process to predict success for RISE! applicants. In addition to paper tests and interviews, we conducted role play and group exercises evaluated by psychologists, our staff, and human resource people from our employer community.

To our surprise, it didn't work. Participants with fewer challenges to overcome frequently dropped out, while participants facing greater challenges persevered. Participants with less of a history of drug problems had a worse graduation rate than those who had been through treatment many times. In addition, the assessment process did not reveal the severity of the problems many applicants were dealing with.

Through experience, we eventually came to understand that perseverance is the most important determinant of whether an applicant will succeed. Before they begin our program, applicants simply cannot understand the enormity of the changes they will need to break the bonds of poverty. They don't know that their basic beliefs, attitudes, and behaviors will need to be completely transformed. No one, to our knowledge, had developed a valid test to predict that level of perseverance.

We decided to stop administering costly tests and instead used an eight-week probationary period as our initial assessment. Now prospective applicants are welcome to try out the program for eight weeks if they meet just the following three conditions:

- Low income (less than $10,000)
- Legal right to work in the United States
- Not a sexual predator or arsonist (criminologists advised us that these groups represent too high a risk)

Final admission to the program depends on both perseverance and the number of earned successes over the probationary period. Our yield from this open-ended, participant-driven selection process is actually slightly better than when we administered a battery of tests.

Our assumption about assessment proved wrong, so we learned from it. We learned that real life—participation in our program—was the best form of assessment. We changed what we were doing and moved on.

This is how learning works in a learning-driven culture. A learning-driven culture is also a culture of experimentation and change. The culture's underlying messages are:

- If it doesn't work, do it differently.
- If it can be improved, do it differently.
- But make change intelligently, using the information and analysis that you gather internally and externally from lessons-learned sessions, research, and evaluation.

In a learning-driven culture, people are encouraged to try new approaches, even if they ultimately fail. Experimentation is seen as an essential way to learn.

When Communicating Results, Find the Right Metaphor

Any time you break new ground, as we have with RISE!, communication becomes more challenging. We experienced great frustration trying to clarify our outcomes-based approach to funders, most of whom insisted on comparing our results to those of more traditional job-training organizations. We recognized we were dealing with that apples-to-oranges problem I noted in Chapter Two: they were comparing other programs' outputs to our outcomes. But how to help potential funders get that point? These were smart, well-meaning people, yet no matter how many times we explained it, for many the message just wasn't getting across.

We first had to learn to let go of our conceptual framework and think about theirs. Their perceptions were based on their experience. From that experience over many years, they had learned what a "job training program" was and how a nonprofit worked. So they put us into a mental pigeonhole called "job training programs" with its related expectations and biases.

If you're going to introduce a new conceptual framework, you need to understand the listener's context. You have to be prepared to repeat your message many, many times, and in different ways, to appeal to the different learning styles of your audience. To help funders understand why our numbers differed from those of traditional organizations, we developed Table 7.1. It provides an apples-to-apples comparison of mission, results, and financial models that helps funders see how different RISE! is from traditional job training programs.

Table 7.1 Business Models: Traditional Job Training Programs Versus RISE!

	Traditional Job Training Model for the Poor	RISE! Model
Mission	Train people and place them in a job above minimum wage	Provide employers with skilled workers, primarily men of color who were once poverty stricken
Results	Number who complete the training program and stay in job for 90 or 180 days Number who are placed in any job	Number who keep a job paying twenty thousand dollars or more with health benefits for one and two years Increased income achieved Recidivism reduction
Characteristics	Short training period, low cost	Long-term training at high investment
Financial model	Cost per person served	Return on investment

The table was a good start and proved quite useful. But what really enabled stakeholders to understand what makes RISE! different was a baseball metaphor I started using. I explained to our stakeholders that RISE!'s goal is to develop as many home run hitters as possible. Not everyone who engages in our program hits a home run. Some become triple hitters, making at least eighteen thousand dollars a year upon exit. Double hitters improve their income by at least 25 percent, and single hitters go from unemployment to employment. But we try not to emphasize anything less than home runs. True, we could easily increase the number of singles, doubles, and triples by relaxing our standards, but we would ultimately hit fewer home runs, thereby undermining our purpose. This metaphor completed the job that the table had begun, and we were home safe (at least most of the time).

Another communications challenge comes from our focus on return on investment rather than the traditional cost-per-person-trained model. We spend more per person than short-term, low-investment training programs do, yet we are sometimes compared to them. Because we have dealt with this issue so frequently, we have learned to develop standards of measuring costs that make more sense for comparison purposes. More important, we've shifted the discussion to explaining value. This has made possible the pay-for-performance payment model we've employed with the state of Minnesota.

We learned to think about this communications challenge from the listener's point of view, to find different ways to communicate our message, and to find the right metaphor. Even so, communication always seems to me a long and arduous process for innovators. When you're challenging the status quo, be prepared for communication challenges to be ever present. Just keep working at it, knowing that it never ends.

In working with government, being right about politics is as important as being right about the issue. In 1995 we began developing a pay-for-performance relationship with Minnesota that ultimately taught us a painful but critical lesson about working with government. We lobbied for a statute, and after it was passed, we benefited from it. The legislation provided a tax credit that a customer company received upon hiring one of our graduates. Here's how it worked for us at RISE!

- The graduate had to go from earning less than ten thousand dollars a year before entering our program to more than twenty thousand dollars with health benefits in the new job.

- The employer could deduct the credit immediately from its next tax payment rather than wait until the end of the tax year.

- If our graduate was still working at the company a year later, the employer would qualify for another tax credit.

- It was up to RISE! to negotiate with employers to pay us the value of the tax credits they received. In times when the economy was strong, we were often able to negotiate an additional payment for the added economic value they were receiving (higher job retention leads to lower turnover expenses).

We liked the tax credit because it tied our customer employers more closely to us, ensured accountability across the board before any money was exchanged, and established an economic basis separate from the whims of annual budget politics.

But in 2000, the Minnesota Department of Revenue began complaining that the paperwork to keep track of the credits was onerous, and they argued that it wasn't a good idea to administer social policy in the tax code. (I didn't know whether to laugh or cry over that comment since the tax code is made up of little else.) The state proceeded to move RISE!'s pay-for-performance payments into a general appropriation that goes to Minnesota's Department of Economic Development. This meant that the money to pay us for meeting the agreed-on performance criteria was now being held in a fund managed by that department. Instead of the customer receiving a tax credit and our then negotiating with the customer to pay us, we now had the right to earn a direct cash payment from the state based on the same outcomes. From our perspective, this arrangement was less than ideal. For one thing, this change removed the customer-employer from the financial transaction. We disagreed with this, since we wanted customers to be aware of the value they were receiving.

The new system had a ceiling to the amount we could be reimbursed for successful RISE! graduates, since it came from specific appropriated funds. If the number of graduates exceeded the number provided for by the appropriation, there was no way we could be remunerated. This happened frequently. When it did, the state couldn't pay us, regardless of our performance, until the following biannual budget cycle, when we would need to lobby once again for a new allocation.

We took stock of the situation: we celebrated what we'd accomplished, let go of what we'd lost, and adapted where we could. We were able to keep the state committed to pay-for-performance, and it continues to be so to this day.

We learned that being right about the issue isn't sufficient. We also had to be right about the politics and the bureaucracy. We learned which groups in the state government were most amenable to our way of doing business. And we learned how to work better with the state. These lessons have come in handy as we continue to lobby for legislation that will support outcomes-based nonprofits in Minnesota.

We have been able to make these dramatic changes because learning and then adapting to what we've learned is business as usual at RISE! We are committed to improving what we do and how we do it, because the principle of being learning driven has been part of our culture since the beginning. Our challenge is to maintain and even strengthen this inquisitive culture as we add more employees and layers of management so we can serve more people.

ONGOING LEARNING

Every successful nonprofit will experience significant reengineering during its lifetime, perhaps many times. To make these changes while minimizing interruption to growth requires you to build a culture from the beginning that focuses on learning from anything that arises. Management and staff are more open to change when you regularly collect intelligence, conduct lessons-learned sessions, and focus on the principles. With that culture, you can more smoothly transform lessons learned into improving what you do and how you do it. Sustaining a learning-driven culture is a continuing challenge, but a highly rewarding one.

QUESTIONS TO HELP YOUR ORGANIZATION BECOME LEARNING DRIVEN

- Are the people in your organization committed to ongoing learning that improves the organization?

- Do you move quickly to try new approaches when something isn't working as well as it might?

- What's the planning process at your organization? Do you ever feel as if you spend more time planning than doing? Or is your organization at the other end of the continuum: you do no planning at all?

- What systems do you have in place for harvesting internal and external intelligence? What would you like to do differently? What are the barriers to that? How can you overcome them?

- If you hired a consultant to help your organization become more learning driven, what would you want the outcomes to be?

- Has your model evolved as the external environment has changed?

8

The Principles in Practice

It's useful to talk about the seven principles one by one, but in real life it doesn't work that way. In real life, organizations become stronger by putting the principles into practice together. In many ways, it's easier to apply them together than individually. Individually each principle is helpful, but collectively, they bring about lasting change. They reinforce each other, working together like a woven rug that, as a whole, is stronger than its individual threads.

The seven principles can make any organization stronger, whatever purpose the organization is dedicated to and regardless of whether things are going well or need to be drastically improved. The principles have practical application outside the issues discussed in this book so far. They can provide a springboard to innovative thinking about how we approach all sorts of endeavors. Simply ask yourself, What if? What if we applied this principle to this problem or issue, where would it lead us? How could it work? You will discover powerful new ways to approach our toughest challenges.

THE SEVEN PRINCIPLES AT WORK IN NONPROFITS AND SOCIAL ENTERPRISE

There's a dynamic relationship among the seven principles as they work together to strengthen an organization. Take the relationship between purpose and measurement. We must measure what counts so that we can determine how well we're meeting the goals of our mission and making progress toward our purpose. When we don't keep purpose in mind, we tend to measure only things that are easier to measure, like inputs and outputs. When we rely on accurate measurement of the wrong things, we are relying on misleading intelligence. This in turn leads to misallocating limited resources, which hampers actual achievement of our mission.

Nonprofits need to practice being market driven, because focusing on the market enables us to understand our customer, pinpoint our strategy more effectively, and create greater social benefit. That increase in social benefit leads to greater economic value since the individual, family, and taxpayer all benefit from higher incomes and lower public costs. In addition, the economic value we create enables us to develop investment vehicles that capitalize our growth so we can better achieve our mission.

Nonprofits must practice and teach specific empowerment skills. Participants need more than good feelings and a sense of self-respect to transform their lives. They (in fact, all of us) need the tools of empowerment, the emotional intelligence that enables individuals to become personally accountable for their future.

Personal accountability makes mutual accountability possible. Every nonprofit must practice mutual accountability to achieve its purpose and mission. I can think of no exceptions. We in the social services sector have a lot of experience with providing entitlements rather than requiring mutual accountability. Experience shows us that entitlements do not produce the long-term, sustainable change in people's lives that nonprofits are seeking.

And finally, being learning driven applies to all the other principles. Successful nonprofits recognize that experimenting, adjusting, and learning from their experience is a continuous process. It takes self-confidence and courage to jump in and learn from outcomes. The leap requires that you learn fast and adjust, but it's well worth the energy. The alternative is overplanning and paralysis, because you're trying too hard to get it right the first time. Our execution of all the principles must be learning driven, so that we become increasingly effective at what we do.

Here are three examples of social-purpose organizations that practice the principles in combination.

College Summit: Refining Its Mission Because of a Lesson in Accountability

College Summit teaches low-income high school students how to apply to and get into college and how to finance that college education. It holds workshops in the summer before senior year to train a core group of students to become peer leaders in this initiative. These leaders play an essential role in transforming the culture of their school into one where many more students strive to go on to postsecondary education. Without them, says founder J. B. Schramm, all the training and coaching that College Summit does in the schools would be perceived by the students as one more thing inflicted on them. With peer leadership, College Summit has a much better chance of getting kids, their parents, and their teachers to put in the work necessary for college admission and finance.

At College Summit's first workshop for thirty-two students at Connecticut College in 1995, an incident occurred that taught Schramm an important lesson: when it comes to communicating the principles of accountability and mission, nothing speaks louder than behavior.

Schramm explains that "ten minutes before it started, one of the teachers came in: 'We have a problem. A few of our students smoked some marijuana on the way up and two of them are having an allergic reaction.'"[1]

Schramm and his colleagues made sure nobody needed to be rushed to the hospital. Then they faced a dilemma:

> We had a code of conduct that the students had signed,
> saying they wouldn't use drugs. The students said, "Well
> we hadn't arrived yet." So, we were thinking, "Wow, do
> we kick out a tenth of the program in the first ten
> minutes? Might this blow the morale of the whole thing?"
> We had no track record. The whole thing could fall
> apart before we had a chance to show them the value

of it. But we made the decision that we would send them home.

We felt that they had given their word, and if we taught them that going to college was more important than keeping their word, we'd be teaching them the wrong thing.

We also knew what kind of program we were. We weren't a program that was about working intensively with kids who needed to work on their boundaries. We were about tapping the power of young people who may have enormous challenges. They have some very tough choices to make. I got up in front of everybody and announced our decision. It was the first thing I said [to the group]. There wasn't a shred of concern in the room. It felt like they were thinking, "Yeah, *we're* serious, *we're* here. Let them go." And that communicated to the students and the staff what we're about.

So College Summit lost some participants, but the enterprise communicated its belief in the principle of accountability to the rest of the group: participants would be held accountable to the conditions they had agreed to.

At the same time, the nonprofit established its own credibility with its participants. If its leaders had allowed the students who got high on the way to the workshop to remain, they would have insulted the students who had chosen to be accountable. And those students would have taken everything else they were taught in the workshop with a huge grain of salt. The act of saying no strengthened their relationship with the participants who were most likely to accomplish their mission: to "increase college enrollment and persistence rates for low-income high school students." It isn't, as Schramm points out, providing in-depth work on rules and boundaries for kids who don't get it. As any parent can tell you, that's an important task. But it isn't the mission that College Summit has chosen, and the incident helped clarify that.

So in the course of one small but critical incident, College Summit clarified its mission, held itself and its participants accountable, and learned the value of saying no as a way of establishing credibility with a critical group of stakeholders.

RISE! Developing Internships Because of a Change in the Market and a Promise to Be Accountable

When you have a learning-driven culture, you can adapt and continue to serve your purpose even when the world you operate in abruptly changes. In the case of RISE! the job market we were used to dried up between 2008 and 2010, so we had to become creative to continue making progress toward achieving our mission.

In the first decade of the twenty-first century, we experienced an economic downturn that economists have called the worst since the Great Depression. This recession led to more layoffs and fewer job opportunities for everyone, including RISE! participants who were ready for full-time employment. If we had simply kept doing what we had been doing, some participants would have become discouraged and reverted to their old lifestyles. Our placement rate would have declined. In addition, our accountability to diligent participants requires us to keep working with them until they get and keep a living-wage job. So instead of reducing our support, we increased our investment by tapping our reserves to pay participants a stipend to work as interns in for-profit and nonprofit organizations. The nonprofits especially were deeply grateful for trained, free (to them) labor during a period when they were forced to lay off employees. At the same time, participants gained valuable experience, increased their competencies, and stayed focused on their future—all of which made them even more market ready as the economy began recovering.

We hadn't instituted internships previously because we hadn't needed to; the job market was strong. But because of the recession, we were reminded that internships are a useful marketing tool for job hunters. Internships express the principle of being market driven. In consumer marketing terms, internships are free samples—a way to "try before you buy." Internships enable job hunters to demonstrate their capabilities for the position in actual work conditions and lower the perceived risk for potential employers. Lowering risk in the hiring process is exactly what most employers are trying to accomplish. That's why they meet with an applicant and look at a résumé to confirm that the applicant has relevant experience.

In the case of RISE! many of our participants have criminal records that make their résumés less appealing to potential employers. The trial period provided by an internship enables employers to evaluate them as they are now, not as they were.

We will rigorously measure the outcomes of this change in our program. As of this writing, participants are already being offered full-time jobs that meet our criteria at the places where they worked as interns. In fact, participants who interned increased their chance for full-time employment by 50 percent. Now that we have seen the clear benefits of internships—keeping participants motivated and engaged so they don't revert to their old lifestyles, making them more experienced and skilled, and establishing employer relationships that lead to full-time jobs—we plan to make paid internships a permanent part of our program.

Measuring what counts told us the effect that the economic downturn was having on our outcomes. Our accountability to our participants meant that we were responsible for coming up with a way to keep them on track, making progress toward getting and keeping a living-wage job. Our learning-driven culture gave us the process to come up with a new way of operating. And being market driven reminded us that internships provide an excellent way for customers to sample the "product" before buying. The principles worked together as they should, and RISE!, our participants, and our customer-employers have all benefited.

RISE! Coaches: Ambassadors of Accountability and Empowerment

At RISE! all of us on the staff do our best to live the seven principles all day and every day. But no one has a greater responsibility to live the principles than our coaches. RISE! coaches are the primary force in helping participants bridge the gap from the world that they have lived in to the world that they aspire to. RISE! participants transform themselves by learning the accountability and empowerment skills that they need to succeed at RISE! and in the workplace. Coaches guide, support, motivate, and provide whatever consequences are needed to enable this transformation to occur.

The coach is a combination teacher-mentor-trouble-shooter and customer relations representative. All participants meet at least once a week to work individually with their assigned coach during their time at RISE! The coach remains the principal contact for graduates through their first year of full-time employment, when their newly acquired empowerment skills can be severely tested.

From the start, coaches have to embody accountability and empowerment as they are practiced at RISE! Their language and behavior introduce the concepts long before anyone takes a class. Every staff member has this responsibility to some extent, but the coach is a participant's most important role model.

The accountability is mutual, of course. Participants hold coaches accountable for providing high-quality, trustworthy guidance. And coaches hold participants accountable for following through on their commitments, despite internal and external obstacles.

Our coaches can't be prescriptive in a standardized way. They deal with diverse participants who present different problems in different ways at different times. They have to be savvy enough to adjust their guidance and their approach on the fly. They have to know enough about each participant to shrewdly assess that person's behavior, advise and encourage, and then hold the person accountable, especially when the excuses come in fast and furious—as they often do in the early stages.

It takes a remarkable person to be a great coach. We've found that coaches need to be savvy, shrewd, and empathetic, but—interestingly—not too sympathetic. In our early days, we had some who failed because they were either too aloof, too prescriptive, or too eager to be traditional caregivers: street-smart participants knew exactly which buttons to push. Through experience, we've gotten good at weeding out such folks before they are hired.

We've found that the success of a coach has more to do with personal qualities than with professional background or education. Some coaches from social services backgrounds have done well, while others were stuck in the caregiving world. Some coaches with business backgrounds have succeeded, while others weren't empathetic enough. And some of our own graduates who have made the difficult transition to self-sufficiency have proven to be terrific coaches after having gained experience working for our customers.

Coaches also have to be comfortable with our market-driven approach. Once a graduate has been placed, the coach becomes a customer relations representative, a critical contact for both the new employee and his or her supervisor. Coaches can reinforce empowerment and accountability skills. They can untangle problems quickly. This keeps our customers happy and our retention rates high.

"What really appealed to our people," says Ron Tortelli, retired senior vice president and head of personnel of SuperValu, "was that when we had someone [from RISE!] placed within our company, the coaches at Twin Cities RISE! would be in contact with our supervisors and with our HR people on a continual basis, inquiring how their graduates were doing. If we had concerns, we were able to contact RISE! coaches to discuss the problem with them and get their advice and support to deal with it."

The reason our coaches work so well and are so highly valued by our customers is that they embody all seven principles. They understand accountability, empowerment, and our market-driven approach. Coaches understand that although they spend most of their time with participants, the employer is the customer. Participants need to be able to meet customer-employers' standards. So coaches must be able to be responsive to the needs of both participants and employers.

Coaches are also extremely aware of the desired outcome: retention. Our mission is to develop employees who not only get but keep that living-wage job. Merely training and placing participants in jobs is not enough. Coaches keep that mission in mind to guide their own activities.

Coaches, more than anyone else, make the principles working together come alive by focusing on our purpose of boosting individuals out of poverty, building participants' sense of accountability, and coaching participants toward personal empowerment. They are also ensuring that we are measuring what counts—retention—and ensuring that the needs of the market—our customer-employers—are met.

Ask any leader of a successful nonprofit about key moments in their experience, and you'll find examples like these—of the principles working together, making the organization better able to achieve its outcomes.

THE PRINCIPLES: PROVEN FOR-PROFIT THINKING
THAT WILL STRENGTHEN ANY NONPROFIT

Nonprofits willingly tackle society's most daunting social problems. They tread where for-profits do not venture, and they do it with fewer resources than the job requires. That's the primary reason that even the largest social-purpose organizations are dwarfed by the enormity of the tasks they face.

These challenges are getting more acute for nonprofits as both state and federal governments reduce their financial support for important social supports that ensure a safe, fair, and secure democracy for all citizens.

Nonprofits need to enlarge their arsenal to cope with these increased challenges. That's where the seven principles come in. They represent proven for-profit thinking that can help any enterprise, for-profit or nonprofit, improve its results and achieve its purpose. Foundations, philanthropists, government officials, and taxpayers all have roles to play since nonprofits cannot take advantage of these principles alone. It requires an open mind, a willingness to foster experimentation, and the courage to change on the part of all stakeholders.

I urge you to incorporate the seven principles into your approach to the challenges you face. They will provide no magic solution to them, but when they are put into practice together, they are a powerful force for change.

What You Can Do to Make a Difference

We are on the threshold of an extraordinarily exciting and challenging time for nonprofit leaders and social entrepreneurs. There's an enormous amount of work to be done. To help you choose your specific course of action, here are some recommendations, grouped by the role you play or you'd like to play in addressing social issues. This list is by no means comprehensive. The recommendations and questions are intended to get you thinking and, most of all, to provoke action.

What Nonprofit Leaders and Social Entrepreneurs Can Do

- *Integrate all the principles.* Ask yourself which of the principles expresses one of your organization's current strengths or one of the strengths that should come easily to your start-up. What's missing? What difference would it make to your organization and your outcomes if you implemented and integrated all the principles? How could each principle improve your enterprise?

- *Develop solutions that can be more sustainable because they're based on economic value.* Start-up capital is somewhat available, as is capital for expanding beyond pilot programs. But an organization that wants to make a meaningful contribution to achieving its broader purpose needs to scale up and become self-sustaining. The key to obtaining capital for that stage of your organization's development lies in measuring outcomes, establishing economic value, and developing mechanisms that recognize the organization's return on investment. For each stakeholder, ask yourself: Who is the beneficiary of the value you create (local, state, or federal government; insurance companies; foundations)? Can you make the economic case to them now? If not, what more information or analysis would you need?

- *Focus on outcomes rather than inputs and outputs.* By tracking the most meaningful data, you can make better decisions about your resource allocation and all of your other strategies and tactics. You can also make a better case with your funders for financial support.

- *Think about mutual accountability.* Are your participants growing in a holistic way from an empowerment perspective? Do they have the belief system they need to sustain permanent behavioral change? Do you practice mutual accountability with each of your stakeholders? If not, how can you establish this relationship?

What Business Leaders Can Do

- *Influence legislative action.* Use your contacts, political action committee contributions, and lobbying ability. Support legislation that creates capital for high-performing nonprofits and holds them accountable.

- *Invest some of your pension money in vehicles that capitalize social benefit and create economic value.* It is important to do this in vehicles that provide a market rate of return on investment—like the human capital performance bond. If we want nonprofits to have the same access to capital that for-profit businesses do, we must provide vehicles with comparable risks and rewards for investors.

- *Provide assistance to social entrepreneurs and nonprofit leaders.* Most nonprofit leaders and social entrepreneurs are more knowledgeable on the program side of their efforts than the economic side. Corporations and their foundations can provide money and know-how to build economic expertise. You can help these leaders learn how to evaluate the value they create, their return on investment, and other elements of the economic case for supporting social good.

- *Provide financial support for social-purpose organizations that are building capacity and going to scale.* As a business leader, you know the value that can be created when a successful small venture goes to scale. Make sure that your philanthropic and investment plans include provision to support nonprofits that are building capacity, not just start-ups and pilot programs.

What Policymakers Can Do

- *Insist on receiving outcomes data from organizations looking for government support.* Be open to organizations including the cost of obtaining such data in their budgets.

- *Demand systems within government to track, capture, and enable rewarding outcomes that encompass economic value.* Developing such systems is critical, but it will not be easy, since government departments are typically tooled up to work with revenue or expenses, but not both.

- *Focus more on return and benefits than costs alone.* Hold spending committees accountable for the return on investment achieved by the programs they fund, not just the cost.

- *Use pay-for-performance approaches.* Pay for performance can ensure that scarce resources are productively deployed and the best providers are appropriately rewarded.

- *Make sure that the outcomes of decisions are aligned with the social interests of society.* For example, the purpose of job training is not merely placement but retention in a better-paying job. The purpose of education is learning and graduation, not merely attending class. Institutions should be held accountable for outcomes that align with social interests—and rewarded accordingly.

What Government Officials Can Do

- *Be open to changes in processes—in decision making, tracking data, and rewarding outcomes.* Bureaucrats often have an aversion to making changes. If society is to be better served, do not resist on the grounds of policy or because start-up costs are significant or because technological changes are required. Creating social good must be the highest priority.

- *Develop ways to track long-term outcomes.* This can be done through the appropriate data, including social security data, while protecting individuals' privacy.

- *Set up mechanisms to capture incremental taxes and cost avoidance.* Accounting systems can be modified to book the benefits by posting increased revenue and decreased expenses to the appropriate budgets, so that actual dollars are captured.

- *Share value creation fairly with the organizations that create it for government.* Support pay-for-performance systems.

What Philanthropists and Philanthropic Organizations Can Do

- *Demand outcomes data from recipients of your philanthropy.* Outcomes data provide these organizations with feedback on how well they are accomplishing their mission and give management an essential tool for deploying resources.

- *Invest your funds—not just what you donate but your actual assets—in market rate social investments that provide a return and are aligned with your social mission.* Put your money where your mouth is. If we want to see nonprofits get access to capital that will enable them to go to scale, as for-profits do, we have to make the investments and find out which financial instruments work best.

- *Provide technical assistance.* Providing assistance to social enterprises, nonprofits, and government will help them establish the mechanisms needed to track outcomes and return on investment.

- *Ensure that your staff members understand the economics of the social investing they do on your behalf—by hiring people who have the knowledge and training any who don't.* Staff members need to provide both the incentive and challenge to nonprofits to make these changes in their thinking and to take action.

- *Support organizations that are leading the way in making these changes.*

What Policy Think Tanks and Civic Organizations Can Do

- *Vet, publicize, and spread the seven principles through conferences, papers, and other communications.*

- *Promote outcomes-based decision making with legislatures and governments.* Outcomes-based decision making is sound fiscal policy that will make social initiatives more effective.

- *Identify and study social issues where these principles can make a difference.* Help social organizations identify opportunities like social problems where the benefit of alleviation is readily quantifiable.

What the Media Can Do

- *Demand the same kind of transparency and accountability from nonprofit results expected from for-profit businesses.*

- *Report on the achievements as well as the missteps of nonprofits and social enterprises.* Apply the same reporting standards to stories of positive outcomes as applied to those of negative outcomes. "Feel good" stories don't have to be superficial. They can inform as well.

- *Look for specific economic value in addition to the human interest angle when reporting stories about social-purpose organizations.* Economic value broadens the reach of the story to public policy, politics, and the long-term well-being of the community. Portions of the public may not care much about specific populations served by nonprofits, but everyone cares how their tax dollars are spent.

- *Have the expertise on staff to understand and interpret outcomes data and return on investment.* You need access to impartial financial expertise to test both the truth of an organization's claim and the relevance of that claim for the public.

- *Hone your ability to explain financial information to the public.* It will make your stories more interesting. Your public will be better able to put your information in context.

What Advocates Can Do

- *Advocate for outcomes-based spending like pay-for-performance systems.*

- *Advocate for new approaches to investing in human services like human capital performance bonds and social impact bonds.*

- *Track the progress of initiatives and innovations.* Then build public awareness of that progress.

What Any Concerned Citizen, Including You, Can Do

- *Reach out to legislators.* By influencing legislators and supporting outcomes-based decision making, you contribute to alleviating our society's social ills.

- *Volunteer with organizations whose purpose you believe in to help them embody the seven principles.* In light of these principles, consider what expertise is lacking in the organizations you support. Can you contribute that expertise yourself or find someone who will?

- *Hold the organizations that you support accountable for their actions.* They will respond by becoming more effective.

- *Donate to organizations that live the seven principles.*

Appendix B

A Note on the Organizations in This Book

The organizations used as examples in this book range from young to long established. They serve local, national, and international communities. They manage money counted in the thousands of dollars to the billions. Here are short descriptions of those featured and of others mentioned as well.

CaringBridge

CaringBridge was founded in 1997 in Eagan, Minnesota, by Sona Mehring, to enable people going through "significant health challenges" to easily build personal Web sites that provide information to a patient's community of loved ones and bring messages of support to the patient. More than 275,000 Web sites have been created. Over half a million people use CaringBridge Web sites daily. Web site authors, visitors, and donors are based throughout the United

States and in more than 225 countries or territories.[1] www.caringbridge.org

College Summit

College Summit was founded in 1993 in Washington, D.C., by J. B. Schramm, an Ashoka fellow (Ashoka is an international society of social entrepreneurs). It works to increase college enrollment among low-income high school students and increase those students' persistence rates (the rate at which they stay in college once they get there). College Summit has an annual budget of more than $20 million. As of 2010, it had served ninety-two thousand students from low-income communities and trained sixteen hundred teachers and principals in its college-going curriculum. It expects to work with thirty-five thousand students in its fiscal 2011–2012 year.[2] www.collegesummit.org

Common Ground/Community Solutions

Common Ground was founded in 1990 in New York City by Rosanne Haggerty, an Ashoka and a MacArthur fellow. The organization works to end homelessness, particularly among the most vulnerable long-term street homeless. It owns and manages almost three thousand units of affordable housing (typically apartments) in New York State and Connecticut that provide tenants with easy access to the multiple support services that many need. It has been a pioneer in outreach to the homeless. Common Ground also works to prevent homelessness in high-risk neighborhoods.[3] In 2011, Haggerty left Common Ground to create a separate nonprofit, Community Solutions, to take Common Ground's work to a national scale. Community Solutions is spearheading the 100,000 Homes campaign, sharing its methods with organizations in ninety U.S. communities with the goal of putting 100,000 homeless people into homes by July 2013. www.commonground.org and www.cmtysolutions.org

Grameen Bank

Since Grameen Bank was formally established in Bangladesh in 1983, it has grown to serve 8.32 million borrowers, 97 percent of whom are women, in 81,372 villages. Loan recovery rate is over 97 percent. According to a Grameen survey, 68 percent of Grameen borrowers' families have crossed the poverty line. Grameen's founder, Muhammad Yunus, was awarded the Nobel Peace Prize in 2006 for his pioneering work in microfinance.[4] www.grameen.com

Habitat for Humanity

Habitat for Humanity was founded in 1976 in Americus, Georgia, by Millard and Linda Fuller. Its primary activity is financing and building houses with volunteer labor, including that of the owners-to-be. Now a worldwide organization with approximately fifteen hundred U.S. affiliates and five hundred international affiliates, its combined total net assets are $2.1 billion. As of 2010, Habitat had built more than 400,000 houses, sheltering more than 2 million people in more than three thousand communities worldwide.[5] www.habitat.org

Jeremiah Program

Jeremiah Program was founded in 1997 in Minneapolis, Minnesota, by Father Michael O'Connell. Jeremiah seeks to break the cycle of poverty by providing on-campus apartments, support services, and training for single mothers with young children. As of 2010, Jeremiah had campuses in Minnesota, North Dakota, and Texas. All Jeremiah women are attending some form of higher education as well as working and raising a family. Jeremiah Program prepares women so they can succeed in the workplace, readies their children for kindergarten, and reduces the family's dependence on public assistance. Jeremiah Program is working to replicate their model nationally. www.jeremiahprogram.org

Lumni

Lumni is a for-profit social enterprise, founded in 2002 in Colombia, to fund higher education through private investment capital. Felipe Vergara, cofounder and CEO, is an Ashoka fellow. Lumni designs and manages social investment funds in the United States, Chile, Colombia, and Mexico that invest in the education of diversified pools of students. This innovative instrument for human capital financing is not an education loan. Rather, the student commits to paying a fixed percentage of his or her income (typically between 4 and 8 percent) for ten years after graduation. Thus, graduates who are unemployed pay nothing during the time without a job. Investors expect to receive a positive return. As of January 2011, Lumni had funded nearly two thousand students with $14 million.[6] www.lumni.net

Minnesota Public Radio

Founded in 1967 by Bill Kling, Minnesota Public Radio began as a single classical music radio station and has grown into a forty-two-station regional network serving over eight million people in the upper midwest. MPR provides news, classical music, and contemporary music programming through traditional radio technology and streaming over the Internet. American Public Media, MPR's parent company, is the nation's second largest distributor of public radio programming, including *A Prairie Home Companion*, hosted by Garrison Keillor. minnesota.publicradio.org

Playworks

Playworks was founded in 1996 in Oakland, California, as Sports4Kids by Jill Vialet, an Ashoka fellow. The organization is dedicated to improving learning in low-income, urban elementary schools through safe, healthy, inclusive, and positive play. Recess is a source of conflict and discipline problems in many schools. Playworks provides a coach to the school whose job is to transform recess and integrate play into the school day, so that students return to class ready to learn. A Playworks operates in twenty-one cities in the United States, serving more than 120,000 students in 320 schools. Students learn conflict resolution techniques in the course of their games and leadership skills through a Junior Coach program. Teachers in many Playworks schools report that after the implementation of the program, they had an average of twenty-four additional hours teaching rather than resolving conflicts and issues that used to spill over from the playground into their classrooms. Playworks has plans for rapid expansion.[7] www.playworks.org

St. Paul Public School System

The St. Paul Public School system serves approximately 42,000 students in the capital city of St. Paul, Minnesota. The district runs sixty-seven different schools, including three alternative schools and one special education school, in addition to elementary, middle, and high schools. Seventy-three percent of the students are students of color, and 69 percent qualify for free or reduced lunch. The principal languages used for school communication are English, Spanish, Hmong, and Somali. www.spps.org/

Twin Cities RISE!

Referred to simply as RISE! throughout this book, Twin Cities RISE! was founded by Steve Rothschild, an Ashoka fellow, in Minneapolis, Minnesota, in 1994. RISE! seeks to end concentrated, multigenerational poverty by providing employers with skilled, reliable employees, primarily men of color. The organization trains participants in a curriculum that takes approximately thirteen months, places them in jobs that pay at least twenty thousand dollars a year with benefits, and coaches them through the first year of their employment. Since 1994 RISE! has grown from a pilot program with nineteen participants to an organization that serves more than fifteen hundred people every year. From 2007 to 2010, RISE! graduates' salaries averaged around twenty-five thousand dollars. www.twincitiesrise.org

The University of Dubuque

Founded in 1852, the University of Dubuque (UD) is a small, private Presbyterian university located in Dubuque, Iowa. UD offers undergraduate, graduate, and theological seminary programs to a student body of approximately 1,600 students. UD states that it is focused on the "intellectual, spiritual, and moral development" of its students. www.dbq.edu

Notes

Introduction

1. The median income in the Twin Cities (the Minneapolis and St. Paul metropolitan areas) was $45,310 in 2007 and $46,087 in 2010.
2. D. Bornstein and S. Davis, *Social Entrepreneurship: What Everyone Needs to Know* (New York: Oxford University Press, 2010).
3. The information for the organizations comes from their respective Web sites.
4. General Mills's charitable leadership was evidenced through the foundation's position as 33rd in giving among all U.S. corporations in 2010, while it was only the 206th largest corporation in revenues. It received numerous awards, including the Harvard Dively Award for corporate social responsibility and a Presidential Citation for Social Responsibility for its ALTCARE venture.

Chapter One

1. U.S. Bureau of the Census, *Current Population Survey*, Historical Poverty Tables, various years, http://www.census.gov/hhes/www/poverty/data/historical/index.html.
2. Ibid.
3. See L. Orr and others, *The National JTPA Study: Impacts, Benefits, and Costs of Title II=A* (Bethesda, Md.: Abt Associates, Mar. 1994).
4. See J. Wallace, *"A Vision for the Workforce Investment System"* (New York: MDRC, Jan. 2007), for a good discussion of federal workforce policies and their consequences. Wallace maintains that workforce

programs (apart from welfare programs) have been targeted toward getting the unemployed into any job, with little regard for a living-wage salary, retention, or advancement, the key requirements of moving up the economic ladder.

5. A 1994 study of federal Jobs Partnership Training Act programs— "*Executive Summary, GAIN Benefits, Costs, and Three-Year Impacts of a Welfare to Work Program*" (New York: MDRC, Sept. 1994)—and other MDRC reports of state welfare-to-work program evaluations, for instance, showed that the average placement wage was only $4,439. After five years of employment, there was less than a 5 percent difference in earnings between those who were given training or placement services and a control group that received no services. MDRC found that most welfare-to-work programs increased individual earnings but lifted few families above the poverty line. Studies of state welfare-to-work programs, some of which provided short-term training and others job search assistance, showed similar results as MDRC concluded a dozen state welfare-to-work programs in 2000 (S. Freedman and others, *Evaluating Alternative Welfare to Work Approaches: Two-Year Impacts for Eleven Programs* [New York: MDRC, June 2000]). Indeed, the average income in the second year of employment was less than $8,000 for the best-performing welfare-to-work site—$3,250 below the poverty line of $11,250 for a family of two in the same year.

6. There is no agreement on what constitutes a living wage, but many practitioners use 200 percent of the federal poverty guideline. The 2011 guidelines vary with family size and geographical location: for a single adult in the forty-eight contiguous states, the guideline is $10,890 and for a family of four, $22,350. Each additional family member adds $3,820.

7. R. Spence and B. Kiel, "*Skilling the Workforce 'On the Cheap': Ongoing Shortfalls in Federal Funding for Workforce Development*" (Washington, D.C.: Workforce Alliance, Sept. 2003).

8. *Digest of Educational Statistics 2005* (Washington, D.C.: National Center for Education Statistics, 2005).

9. For more on situational versus generational poverty, see R. Payne, *A Framework for Understanding Poverty* (Highlands, Tex.: aha! Process, 2005).

10. Brookings Institution Metropolitan Policy Program, *Mind the Gap: Reducing Disparities to Improve Regional Competitiveness in the Twin Cities* (Washington, D.C.: Brookings Institution, 2005).

11. Ibid.

12. "Newly released figures from the U.S. Bureau of Labor Statistics place Minnesota's 2010 black jobless rate at 22 percent. That's 3.4 times the white rate of 6.4 percent, giving the state the largest gap in the country. A 2009 analysis by the Economic Policy Institute found that among 18 of the largest metro areas, the Twin Cities had the biggest gap between white and black unemployment. The state's black population is concentrated in the Twin Cities." "Twin Cities Jobless Gap Worst in Nation," *Star Tribune*, Mar. 23, 2011.

13. Interview with F. Vergara, cofounder and CEO of Lumni, Jan. 18, 2011.

14. V. Frankl, *Man's Search for Meaning* (1946).

15. F. Nietzsche, *Twilight of the Idols* (1889).

Chapter Two

1. The Ten Indicators of Grameen Bank, http://www.grameen-info.org /index.php?option=com_content&task=view&id=792&Itemid=759, slightly edited to correct translation, accessed Nov. 2, 2010.

2. "Lessons Learned over a Quarter of a Century," http://www.grameen -info.org.

3. The gold standard of evaluation involves comparing a group that is treated in a program with an untreated control group. Some researchers argue that such a counterfactual study is necessary to determine the true incremental effect of a particular intervention. RISE! hasn't completed a formal counterfactual study, but we have compared our recidivism reduction results to the dropouts from our program to determine the 66% reduction rate. A counterfactual study

is planned for the Human Capital Performance Bond pilot discussed in Chapter Six.

Chapter Three

1. Interview with Sona Mehring, Dec. 1, 2010.
2. See D. Bornstein, "Hard Times for Recess," NYTimes.com, Apr. 4, 2012, http://opinionator.blogs.nytimes.com/2011/04/04 /hard-times-for-recess.
3. Ibid.
4. "Playworks Impact," n.d., http://www.playworks.org/files/Playworks _Impact.pdf.

Chapter Four

1. Interview with J. Reckford, CEO, Habitat for Humanity International, Dec. 17, 2010.
2. This is the model for Habitat for Humanity International and its more than fifteen hundred affiliates in the United States. Internationally, Habitat is experimenting with other ways of operating that fit within its purpose and mission: for example, microloans to enable the very poor to make an individual home improvement, like a roof or a floor. In a disaster situation, like the 2004 Indian Ocean tsunami or the 2010 Haitian earthquake, Habitat may supply basic shelter without requiring sweat equity. In some of these instances, Habitat may charge very low interest, rather than no interest, which is its basic practice.
3. Interview with V. Goldsmith, executive director, Habitat for Humanity of Cape Cod.
4. For the Fund for Humanity's mission statement, see "History of Habitat," http://www.habitat.org/how/historytext.aspx?print=true. The Fund for Humanity was created in 1968 by those who later created Habitat for Humanity.

Chapter Five

1. "Emotional Intelligence," June 8, 2011, http://en.wikipedia.org/wiki /Emotional_intelligence.

2. See "The Case for Emotional Intelligence," http://www.6seconds.org /case/.

3. Definition adapted from http://en.wikipedia.org/wiki/Cognitive _behavioral_therapy. Wikipedia's definition is based on British Association for Behavioral and Cognitive Psychotherapies, "What Is CBT?" http://www.babcp.com/Public/What_is_CBT.aspx.

4. R. Payne, *A Framework for Understanding Poverty*. (4th rev. ed.) (Highlands, Tex.: aha! Process, 1996).

5. The use of alphabets and formulas to express these ideas has many precedents in the fields of cognitive psychology. Psychologist Albert Ellis, founder of rational emotive therapy, used an ABC model: A (activating event) + B (beliefs), leads to C (consequences). In his book, Martin Seligman varies the ABC model so that A = adversity. M. Seligman, *Learned Optimism* (New York: Knopf, 1991). In *The Success Principle* (New York: HarperCollins, 2006), Jack Canfield uses $E + R = O$ (Event + Response = Outcome). At RISE! we have found $E + R^{(B)} = O$ to be the most useful way to make the point to our participants.

6. According to John Stewart, the University of Dubuque has deliberately decided that it is in the business of formational education, that is, training students in values and behaviors that another institution might leave to family and church. The university is definitely acting in loco parentis. For example, faculty take attendance at class and follow up with students who are experiencing difficulties, to the extent of knocking on their dorm room door. It considers empowerment training part of that intrusive programming to teach values.

Chapter Six

1. For a good definition of the discount rate, go to http://www .valuadder.com/glossary/discount-rate.html.

2. The discount rate is the interest rate used in discounted cash flow analysis to determine the present value of future cash flows. The discount rate takes into account the time value of money (the idea that money available now is worth more than the same amount of

money available in the future because it could be earning interest) and the risk or uncertainty of the anticipated future cash flows (which might be less than expected). See http://www.valuadder.com/glossary /discount-rate.html for more information.

3. Government general obligation bonds are a common type of municipal bond in the United States that is secured by a state or local government's pledge to use legally available resources, including tax revenues, to repay bondholders. A revenue bond is a special type of municipal bond distinguished by its guarantee of repayment solely from revenues generated by a specified revenue-generating entity associated with the purpose of the bonds, rather than from a tax.

4. Social Finance, "Social Finance Launches First Social Impact Bond," press release, Sept. 2010.

5. Ibid.

6. Social Finance, "Social Impact Bonds: Rethinking Finance for Social Outcomes," Aug. 2009, http://www.socialfinance.org.uk/sites/default /files/SIB_report_web.pdf.

7. A bond is a debt security in which the authorized issuer owes the holders a debt and, depending on the terms of the bond, is obliged to pay interest (the coupon) to use or to repay the principal at a later date, termed maturity. A bond is a formal contract to repay borrowed money with interest at fixed intervals.

8. "Social Finance Launches First Social Impact Bond," Social Finance press release, Mar. 18, 2011, http://www.socialfinance.org.uk/news /press-releases/social-finance-launches-first-social-impact-bond.

9. Rating services rate bonds based on their risk. The best is AAA, and the worst are junk bonds. As the rating falls to indicate increased risk, the interest rate goes up. AAA government bonds are backed by the full faith and credit of the state. The human capital performance bond is AA, higher risk and lower rated than AAA, but still relatively safe.

Chapter Seven

1. M. Yunus, "Lessons Learnt over a Quarter of a Century," n.d., http:// www.grameen-info.org/index.php?option=com_content&task=view&id =30&Itemid=764.

2. A. Counts, *Small Loans, Big Dreams: How Nobel Prize Winner Muhammad Yunus and Microfinance Are Changing the World* (Hoboken, NJ: Wiley, 2008).

3. Ibid.

4. A. Guice, "Redesigning Urban Classrooms to Impact Student Achievement," *International Journal of Educational Leadership Preparation*, 2009, 4(2), http://cnx.org/content/m21052/latest/.

Chapter Eight

1. Interview with J. B. Schramm, founder and CEO, College Summit, Dec. 9, 2010.

Appendix B

1. Interview with Sona Mehring, founder and CEO; www.caringbridge .org; Caring Bridge 2009 *Annual Report*; materials supplied by CaringBridge; and D. Logeland and J. Rash, "CaringBridge Comes of Age in an Age of Social Media," *Twin Cities Business*, Dec. 2010, http://www.tcbmag.com/peoplecompanies/features/133540p3.aspx.

2. Interview with J. B. Schramm, founder and CEO, and Vanessa Lillie, public relations and communications manager; D. Bornstein, *How to Change the World* (New York: Oxford University Press, 2007); "College Summit," case study N-9-308-088 (Boston: Harvard Business School, 2008); R. Buckman, "If Gordon Gekko Had a Good Heart, This Is How He Might Have Done It," *Wall Street Journal*, May 16, 2006; www.collegesummit.org.

3. Interview with Rosanne Haggerty, president; A. Parsons, "Mini Case Study: How Common Ground Reinvented Its Homelessness Strategy," dowser.org, May 11, 2010, http://www.commonground .org/?p=4146; D. Bornstein, "A Plan to Make Homelessness History," *New York Times*, Dec. 20, 2010; D. Bornstein, "The Street Level Solution," Jan. 3, 2011, *New York Times*; www.commonground .org.

4. A. Counts, *Small Loans, Big Dreams* (Hoboken, N.J.: Wiley, 2008); D. Bornstein and S. Davies, *Social Entrepreneurship: What Everyone Needs to Know* (New York: Oxford University Press, 2008); C. Bruck,

"Millions for Millions," *New Yorker*, Oct. 30, 2006; www
.grameen.com.

5. Interviews with Jonathan Reckford, CEO, Habitat for Humanity
International, and Victoria Goldsmith, executive director, Habitat for
Humanity of Cape Cod; S. Ramage. "He'd Like to Build the World a
Home," *Stanford Magazine*, Nov.–Dec. 2006; M. Fuller, *No More
Shacks! The Daring Vision of Habitat for Humanity* (Nashville, Tenn.:
Thomas Nelson, 1986).

6. Interview with Felipe Vergara, cofounder and CEO; "Felipe Vergara
and Lumni: Launching an Innovation in a Developing Economy,"
case study (Charlottesville: University of Virginia, 2006); "America's
Most Promising Social Entrepreneurs: Lumni," *Business Week*, Apr. 3,
2009; "Making the Grade: Funding Poor Students Could Be the Next
Big Thing in Microfinance," *Economist*, Sept. 9, 2010.

7. Interview with Jill Vialet, president and founder; D. Bornstein, "Hard
Times for Recess," *New York Times*, Apr. 4, 2011; www.playworks.org.

Acknowledgments

This book—and Twin Cities RISE!—would not have been possible without the assistance of and contributions from many individuals.

Michael Patton, an extraordinary evaluator and thinker, helped in the early development of RISE! and this book.

Michael O'Keefe and Carol Berde, formerly president and vice president, respectively, of the McKnight Foundation, and Terry Saario, former president of the Northwest Area Foundation, encouraged the development of RISE! with their challenging questions and significant early seed money.

I thank my good friend Bill George, who not only encouraged this effort but set such an extraordinary example for me as a businessman, teacher, and successful author.

Scott Edelstein helped me restructure the book when it was needed, and Joan Oliver Goldsmith did a magnificent job of assisting me in researching, rewriting, and editing the manuscript.

Cy Yusten, of Twin Cities RISE!, provided his expertise to Chapter Five on personal empowerment.

Chuck Denny, Verne Johnson, Penny George, Mike Bingham, Anita Pampusch, Mitch Pearlstein, Jodi Sandfort, Rob Sayre, Joe Selvaggio, Neal St. Anthony, Bill Svrluga, Susan Walen, the late Tom McBurney, Zack Rothschild, and Mary Bednarowski provided valuable insights. I also thank Bill Gladstone, my agent, for his belief in the project, and Karen Murphy, my editor, and the Jossey-Bass team for their guidance and support. I thank the many past and present employees of Twin Cities RISE! whose passion, commitment, and intelligence have made a difference in so many lives, and to the graduates whose courage and persistence inspire me.

Finally, I thank my wife, Marilyn, for her unwavering support for my many nonprofit endeavors over the past twenty years and her encouragement for writing a book to share what I have learned.

About the Author

Steve Rothschild is a successful social entrepreneur and businessman. He founded, chairs, and was CEO of Twin Cities RISE!, a unique antipoverty program for very low-income adults, especially African American men, for living-wage jobs. Its combination of remedial education, skills training, and personal empowerment develops the whole person. He also founded and is president of Invest in Outcomes, a nonprofit that created the human capital performance bond, a new source of capital for high-performing nonprofit organizations that is being piloted by the State of Minnesota. Earlier, he successfully launched Yoplait, USA, serving as its first president, and then was executive vice president of General Mills. He has served on numerous for-profit and nonprofit boards. Rothschild is an Ashoka fellow, a fellowship of leading social entrepreneurs. He can be reached at steverothschild.org.

Index